The Womb of My Heart
Rosary Devotional

Laura Ercolino

En Route Books and Media, LLC
Saint Louis, MO

⊕ ENROUTE
Make the time

En Route Books and Media, LLC
5705 Rhodes Avenue
St. Louis, MO 63109

Contact us at
contactus@enroutebooksandmedia.com

Cover Credit: 13th-century icon of the Great Panagia
(Our Lady of the Sign) from the Saviour Minster
in Yaroslavl, Russia

Copyright 2025 Laura Ercolino

ISBN-13: 979-8-88870-452-3
Library of Congress Control Number:
Available online at https://catalog.loc.gov

Table of Contents

The Sorrowful Mysteries

The Glorious Mysteries

Introduction

"If there is only one mother of Christ according to the flesh, all are begetting Christ according to the faith." St. Ambrose

The Annunciation and Incarnation in Nazareth was a historical moment. God entered human existence, married His Divinity to our humanity, and brought eternity into time, all in and through the Blessed Virgin Mary.

In a particular historical moment, Immaculate Mary gave birth to God-With-Us, to the Incarnate Jesus. Each of us is chosen and called to spiritually give birth to Jesus, again and again. A spiritual annunciation, incarnation, and nativity occurs every time we give our "Fiat" to the will of God, and the love of Christ is made visible in our corner of the world, our relationships, and our little piece of eternity.

In the Byzantine tradition, the virginal womb of our Blessed Mother has been so beautifully described as "the womb more spacious than the heavens" for it contained the Creator of all that exists. If our hearts are to have room for Jesus, we must surrender to His gentle healing, purifying, and stretching of our hearts. Our hearts must become more and more like Mary's virginal womb - pure, available, and receptive.

In 2023, as I was preparing to make a private vow of spiritual marriage to Christ the Bridegroom, I asked the Blessed Mother how I should pray in order to prepare my heart for Him. She gently led me back to a memory from years before when I had been grieving the loss of my fertility due to a medically necessary hysterectomy. One particular day during this time, I was alone in my parish church praying the Joyful Mysteries of the Rosary. I began to sob as I pondered how Mary had opened her heart and body to the Holy Spirit and Love Himself became incarnate within her. I cried out to her that I couldn't give myself to Him like that anymore. In the very depths of my being, I sensed her saying, "Let your heart be a womb where He can be born anew."

As these words came back to me, I was inspired to write and pray this Womb of My Heart Rosary. This Rosary continues to deepen my own understanding of the unique way the Father invites each of us to participate in the eternal and spiritual annunciation and incarnation event. I desire to offer my heart to Him - purified, available, and receptive - a virginal womb, in which the love of Christ may be birthed anew into this time and place, into the lives of those whom He entrusts to me.

I have written this Rosary devotional in such a way that you can use it again and again. In the different seasons of our lives, it is fruitful to return to a past devotion and allow the Lord to bear new fruit. The Rosary, when prayed from the heart, will always bear good fruit. Secondly, this devotional is not just a guide to the contemplative Rosary. In this book, you will find twenty-five days of food for your heart - Scripture passages, Wisdom from the Saints, reflections, questions to ponder, sacred art for contemplation, as well as Rosary meditations and prayers. The banquet of rich spiritual food may seem overwhelming. Do not be afraid. Let the Holy Spirit guide your prayer by savoring the parts of this devotional that resonate with you, leaving the rest for another time.

I have focused on one Mystery of the Rosary each day. I guide you in pondering and praying each Mystery on its own. The purpose of this is to help you enter more deeply into the lives of Jesus and Mary. We learn the art of pondering the mysteries of the Christ-life from the Blessed Mother who St. Luke tells us treasured and pondered in her heart the events of her life with Jesus.(See Luke 2:19 and 2:51).The events we remember in the Holy Rosary, like the Annunciation, are historical events, yet the Father is continually inviting us to spiritually participate in those events. By contemplating the Mysteries of the Holy Rosary, we will begin to see that God is "re-living" the Christ-life within our own lives. It is my hope that through the meditations and prayers in this devotional, you will begin to recognize the Christ-life alive in you.

May praying this Rosary bring you joy and courage as you, too, make a womb of your heart for our dear Savior, Jesus Christ.

Together in His Heart,

Laura Ercolino,
Foundress of Hope's Garden

Day 1

The Rosary and the Life of Christ in Me

Scripture: Matthew 12:50, Galatians 4:19

"For whoever does the will of my Father in heaven is my brother and sister and mother."

"My little children, for whom I am again in the pain of childbirth until Christ is formed in you…"

Wisdom from the Saints

"God the Holy Ghost, being barren in God-that is to say, not producing another Divine Person - is become fruitful by Mary, whom He has espoused. It was with her, in her, and of her that He produced His Masterpiece, which is God made Man, and that He goes on producing daily, to the end of the world, the predestinate and the members of the Body of that adorable Head. This is the reason why He, the Holy Ghost, the more He finds Mary, His dear and inseparable spouse in any soul, the more active and mighty He becomes

in producing Jesus Christ in that soul, and that soul in Jesus Christ." - St. Louis de Montfort

"The Rosary, though clearly Marian in character, is at heart a Christocentric prayer. ... It has all the depth of the Gospel message in its entirety, of which it can be said to be a compendium. With the Rosary, the Christian people sit at the school of Mary and are led to contemplate the beauty on the face of Christ and to experience the depths of his love." - St. John Paul II

Reflection

The Rosary is far more than a series of prayers recited by heart; it is a profound way of entering into meditation and contemplation. Through its rhythm of *Our Fathers, Hail Marys,* and *Glory Bes,* the Rosary invites us to "be still and know" God (cf. Psalm 46:10). Like a gentle and rhythmic heartbeat calms a child held to its mother's breast, the repetition of these prayers calms the mind and creates space for the mysteries of Christ's life to unfold in the imagination and the heart. Each decade of the Rosary is centered on a Mystery drawn from the Gospels: the joyful moments of Christ's birth and childhood, the luminous or light-giving events of His public ministry, the sorrowful scenes of His Passion, the triumph of His Resurrection and the glorious destiny of the Blessed Virgin and every faithful soul. As we ponder these Mysteries in the lives of Jesus and Mary, our prayer becomes a form of sacred storytelling, a means of re-telling the story of Jesus and Mary's life together intertwined with our own.

Prayed contemplatively, the Rosary draws us into mystical union with Jesus and Mary, opens the door to the womb of our hearts, and allows the Christ-life to take root and blossom within our lives. St. John Paul II was devoted to the Rosary and taught us that the Rosary is a school of contemplation. He wrote that "to recite the Rosary is nothing other than to contemplate with Mary the face of Christ." Each bead, each Hail Mary, becomes an anchor for the mind and we are led into deeper silence and communion with God. Praying the Rosary as St. John Paul II teaches is less about saying prayers and more about praying from the heart. In this way, the contemplative Rosary leads us into encounters with Christ that transform our hearts and lives.

When prayed slowly and attentively, the Rosary draws us in Mary's footsteps which always lead to intimacy with Jesus. The Bride's prayer in the Song of Songs becomes our own, "Draw us in your footsteps, let us run!" (Song of Songs 1:3). If this is our reason for praying the Rosary, then we must change the way we pray it. Just as the birth of a new baby requires nine months of hidden silence in darkness, the building of an intimate relationship and the transformation of the heart require patient endurance.

The analogies of the natural birthing and mothering process and the nuptial imagery of the Song of Songs may seem uncomfortable to you. These are the very analogies that God chose. In many Scriptures, God refers to Himself as the Spouse or Husband of His people (see Isaiah 54:5 and 62:4-5, Jeremiah 3:14, Hosea 2:16, 19-20, Ezekiel 16:8), and Jesus refers to Himself as the Bridegroom, (see Mark 2:19-20, Matthew 25:1-13, Matthew 22:1-14). In the New Testament, St. Paul continues the use of the nuptial analogy to describe how Christ loves His Bride the Church (see Ephesians 5:25-27; 2 Corinthians 11:12). And in Revelation, St. John describes Heaven as the eternal wedding feast of the Lamb and the New Jeru-salem as the Bride (Revelation 19:7-10; 21:2). Look-ing at the Bible as a whole, it becomes evident that God wants to marry us - "us" as in the whole of His creation and "us" as in each individual human per-son.

The image of spiritual motherhood also echoes throughout the Old and New Testaments. In the Old Testament, through the prophets Moses, Isaiah, and Hosea, God describes His love and care for His Cho-sen People with maternal imagery. Below are a few examples.

"You were unmindful of the Rock that bore you; you forgot the God who gave you birth." (Deuter-onomy 32:18)

"Can a woman forget her nursing child, or show no compassion for the child of her womb? Even these may forget, yet I will not forget you." (Isaiah 49:15)

"As a mother comforts her child, so I will comfort you; you shall be comforted in Jerusalem." (Isaiah 66:13)

"Did I conceive all this people? Did I give birth to them, that you should say to me, 'Carry them in your bosom, as a nurse carries a sucking child,' to the land that you promised on oath to their ancestors?" (Numbers 11:12)

"Yet it was I who taught Ephraim to walk, I took them up in my arms; but they did not know that I healed them. I led them with cords of human kindness, with bands of love. I was to them like those who lift infants to their cheeks. I bent down to them and fed them." (Hosea 11:3–4)

Jesus uses maternal imagery to describe His love for Jerusalem in Matthew 23:37 and Luke 13:34. St. Paul also makes use of this analogy to describe how he cares for and nurtures the "infant" Christian community.

"But we were gentle among you, like a nurse tenderly caring for her own children." (1 Thessalonians 2:7)

"My little children, for whom I am again in the

pain of childbirth until Christ is formed in you…"
(Galatians 4:19)

"Like newborn infants, long for the pure, spiritual
milk, so that by it you may grow into salvation—
if indeed you have tasted that the Lord is good."
(1 Peter 2:2–3)

The Church confirms and clarifies the teaching
of Scripture. There are too many examples to cite
them all here. These are a few statements about the
nuptial mystery at the heart of our faith and the
motherhood of the Church that I have found most
helpful to contemplate.

> *"The entire Christian life bears the mark of the
> spousal love of Christ and the Church. Already
> Baptism, the entry into the People of God, is a nup-
> tial mystery; it is so to speak the nuptial bath which
> precedes the wedding feast, the Eucharist." Cate-
> chism of the Catholic Church #1617*

> *"To be loved by Christ and to love him with spousal
> love is constitutive of the Church's mystery." Pope
> John Paul II, General Audience, Feb. 7, 2001*

"We find ourselves at the very heart of the Paschal Mystery, which completely reveals the spousal love of God. Christ is the Bridegroom because 'he has given himself': his body has been 'given,' his blood has been 'poured out'... As the Redeemer of the world, Christ is the Bridegroom of the Church. The Eucharist is the Sacrament of the Bridegroom and of the Bride. The Eucharist makes present and re-alizes anew ... the redemptive act of Christ ... Christ is united with this 'body' as the bridegroom with the bride." Pope John Paul II, Mulieris Digni-tatem (Apostolic Letter, 1988)

"God's love for man ... is also a love where 'God's very Heart, the Almighty, awaits the 'yes' of his creatures as a young bridegroom that of his bride.'" Pope Benedict XVI, Homily March 29, 2007

"The Church is your mother; she gave you birth in baptism. The Church nourishes you with the milk of her sacraments." St. Augustine, Sermon 57, On the Creed

"The Church is a mother, not only bringing forth children but nourishing them with her own milk.

She brings them to maturity through the preaching of the word." St. John Chrysostom

"The Church is our mother because she gives us new life in Christ and brings us up in the faith. Like a mother, she nourishes us with the sacraments and teaches us with tenderness." Pope St. John Paul II, General Audience, September 1991

"The Church is also a mother: she gives us new life in Christ and accompanies us with care, with love, with the tender care of a mother." Pope Benedict XVI, General Audience, January 2009

St. John Paul II described authentic love as having four necessary qualities. Spousal love must be total, free, faithful, and fruitful. If this is true for human married love, how true it must be for our relationship with Christ. As we grow in intimacy with Christ, the Bridegroom of our souls, our lives "birth" His presence anew and He leads us into roles of "mothering" and forming souls. As members of His Bride and the Mother of Humanity, we too are called to spiritual brideship and spiritual motherhood, just as St. Paul was. Remember, we are speaking of spiritual realities!

As I wrote in the Introduction, I began praying the Womb of My Heart Rosary as I prepared to make a private vow of spiritual marriage to Christ the Bridegroom. I was struck by the fact that my earthly marriage had been very fruitful; God blessed me with nine beautiful children. How much more fruitful would Christ then make my spiritual marriage to Himself? I began asking myself and Mother Mary, "Am I really ready for all that it means to be His bride? Am I prepared to give myself to Him totally, freely, faithfully, and to allow Him to be fruitful through me?"

These are not just questions that someone discerning a private or religious vow needs to ponder. In Deuteronomy 6 and again in Luke 10:27, God instructs all Christians with this commandment, "You shall love the Lord your God with all your heart, and with all your soul, and with all your might."; "You shall love the Lord your God with all your heart, and with all your soul, and with all your strength, and with all your mind; and your neighbor as yourself.".

Before you begin this journey with Jesus and Mary through the Mysteries of the Holy Rosary and ask that your heart be made like unto her virginal womb, take time to ponder these questions. Contemplate the Scriptures cited above and the truths of our faith as quoted from the Saints and the *Catechism of the Catholic Church*. The purifying, emptying, and transforming of our hearts into wombs offered to God is the path to loving Him with our whole self just as Mary does and did at the moment of the Annunciation. He will answer our prayer and our lives will birth the light and love of Christ anew for the life of the world.

Questions for Journaling and Reflection

- What has been my experience of praying the Rosary up until now?
- What has been my relationship with Mother Mary up until now? What do I desire my relationship with her to be like? Can I identify the fears or obstacles to my having the relationship I desire?
- Write your own prayer to Mother Mary. Pray from your heart with honesty and vulnerability. Tell her about your desires and your fears

as you begin praying this Womb of My Heart Rosary.

13th-century icon of the Great Panagia (Our Lady of the Sign) from the Saviour Minster in Yaroslavl, Russia

The Joyful Mysteries

Annunciation of Ustyug
Russian Icon written in Novgorod
Artist Unknown (1120-1140)

Day 2 - The Joyful Mysteries

The First Joyful Mystery:
The Annunciation

Scripture: Luke 1: 26-38

"In the sixth month the angel Gabriel was sent by God to a town in Galilee called Nazareth, to a virgin betrothed to a man named Joseph, of the House of David; and the virgin's name was Mary. He went in and said to her, 'Rejoice, you who enjoy God's favor! The Lord is with you.' She was deeply disturbed by these words and asked herself what this greeting could mean, but the angel said to her, 'Mary, do not be afraid; you have won God's favour. Look! You are to conceive in your womb and bear a son, and you must name him Jesus. He will be great and will be called Son of the Most High. The Lord God will give him the throne of his ancestor David; he will rule over the House of Jacob for ever and his reign will have no end.' Mary said to the angel, 'But how can this come about, since I have no knowledge of man?' The angel answered,

'The Holy Spirit will come upon you, and the power of the Most High will cover you with its shadow. And so the child will be holy and will be called Son of God. And I tell you this too: your cousin Elizabeth also, in her old age, has conceived a son, and she whom people called barren is now in her sixth month, for nothing is impossible to God.' Mary said, 'You see before you the Lord's servant, let it happen to me as you have said.' And the angel left her."

Wisdom from the Saints

"The world being unworthy to receive the Son of God immediately from the hands of the Father, He gave His Son to Mary for the world to receive Him from her." - St. Augustine

"Even her maternal relationship would have done Mary no good unless she had borne Christ more happily in her heart than in her flesh." - St. Augustine

Reflection

Mary's 'yes' to God, through the angel Gabriel, was a total and complete gift of self: the response of a Bride to her Bridegroom. God did not force her assent or steal her gift. He invited; He asked; He wooed her with His lovingkindness. Mary's fiat was not a timid resignation or a fear motivated consent. Rather, she responded to the love of God with a bold display of trust and openness. Love - authentic love - must first and foremost be free. If it is not freely and willingly given, it cannot be total, faithful, and fruitful.

God invites us to imitate Mary's receptivity, responsiveness to His love, and fearless trust in His will. Mary models for us a bridal posture in prayer, the posture of openness and receptivity to the Love to which all souls are invited. The Father desires to overshadow each of us with His Holy Spirit and for His Son, Christ, to find a dwelling place in our hearts.

Questions for Journaling and Reflection

- Where is God inviting me to say 'yes' right now?
- What wounds or insecurities cause me to close my heart or fear imitating the receptivity and openness of Mary?
- Am I in the habit of asking God what He needs me to do rather than letting the Holy Spirit "do unto me according to His word"?

Rosary Prayer (One Decade)

Opening Prayer: Come Holy Spirit, Sweet Spouse of the Blessed Virgin Mary and Spouse of my soul. Purify and prepare my heart to be a virginal womb in which Divine Love may grow. May Jesus find His place of rest and delight here in the womb of my heart. Amen.

Apostles' Creed
Our Father
3 Hail Marys

Hail Mary full of grace, the Lord is with thee. Blessed art thou amongst women and blessed is the fruit of thy womb, Jesus. Holy Mary, Mother of God, **make my heart like unto thy virginal womb**, and pray for us sinners now and at the hour of our death. Amen.

Glory Be

The First Joyful Mystery: The Annunciation

Prayer: Come Holy Spirit and plant the seeds of Divine Love in the womb of my heart. Water my Beloved's garden with dew drops of grace. May His love blossom and grow within me. Amen.

> *"I sleep, but my heart is awake. I hear my Beloved knocking. 'Open to me, my sister, my love, my dove, my perfect one, for my head is covered with dew, my locks with the drops of night.'" Song of Songs 5:2*

Our Father, 10 Hail Marys

Hail Mary full of grace, the Lord is with thee. Blessed art thou amongst women and blessed is the fruit of thy womb, Jesus. Holy Mary, Mother of God, **make my heart like unto thy virginal womb**, and pray for us sinners now and at the hour of our death. Amen.

Glory Be, Fatima Prayer

Closing Prayer:

Jesus, Sweet Spouse of my soul, I open the womb of my heart to You. Come and enter Your enclosed garden with the same incarnate love with which You entered the immaculate womb of Your Blessed Mother. In me, with me, and through me, bring the joy of Your Divine Love to birth again today. Amen.

The Visitation
St. Sophia of Kyiv
Artist: Unknown (circa 1000)

Day 3 - The Joyful Mysteries

The Second Joyful Mystery:
The Visitation

Scripture: Luke 1: 39-56

"Mary set out at that time and went as quickly as she could into the hill country to a town in Judah. She went into Zechariah's house and greeted Elizabeth. Now it happened that as soon as Elizabeth heard Mary's greeting, the child leapt in her womb and Elizabeth was filled with the Holy Spirit. She gave a loud cry and said, 'Of all women you are the most blessed, and blessed is the fruit of your womb. Why should I be honoured with a visit from the mother of my Lord? Look, the moment your greeting reached my ears, the child in my womb leapt for joy. Yes, blessed is she who believed that the promise made her by the Lord would be fulfilled.' And Mary said: My soul proclaims the greatness of the Lord and my spirit rejoices in God my Saviour; because he has looked upon the humiliation of his servant. Yes, from now onwards all generations will call me blessed, for the Almighty has done

great things for me. Holy is his name, and his faithful love extends age after age to those who fear him. He has used the power of his arm, he has routed the arrogant of heart. He has pulled down princes from their thrones and raised high the lowly. He has filled the starving with good things, sent the rich away empty. He has come to the help of Israel his servant, mindful of his faithful love -according to the promise he made to our ancestors - of his mercy to Abraham and to his descendants for ever. Mary stayed with her some three months and then went home."

Wisdom from the Saints

"The more one loves God, the more one loves people. The love of God, the love of people, is my whole life". - Bl. Charles de Foucauld

"It is to be noted that the Word, the Son of God, together with the Father and the Holy Spirit, essentially and personally remain hidden in the inmost center of the soul." - St. John of the Cross

Reflection

Mary's first act after receiving Christ was to go out in joyful charity. The Bridegroom within her compelled her to love her neighbor. Mary, just like the Bride of the Song of Songs, experienced the truth that the love of Christ cannot be contained. Love, authentic love, is always total, free, faithful and *fruitful*. When Love Himself was but a tiny embryo within her womb, Mary carried Him to her cousin in need. She shared not only her helping hands but also her heart that was now one with the Heart of God.

The Blessed Virgin had become a living tabernacle - the dwelling place of God-With-Us. St. Elizabeth and the babe in her womb recognized Emmanuel's hidden presence and rejoiced. Jesus promises that all who love Him will become His dwelling places, living tabernacles. *"Jesus answered him, 'If anyone loves me, he will keep my word, and my Father will love him, and we will come to him and make our home with him'" (John 14:23).*

The presence of Christ instills a profound and contagious joy such as the Bride of the Song expresses in her exclamation, *"Draw me in your footsteps, let us run!"* (Song of Songs 1:4). True love of God must lead to true love of our neighbors, all those whom He entrusts to us. May Mother Mary teach us how to bring the gift of the Bridegroom to those in need of His love.

Questions for Journaling and Reflection

- Who is God calling me to 'visit' with His love?
- How does Christ's presence within me bring joy to others?
- In what ways can I be more aware of the truth that I am a living Tabernacle carrying Jesus hidden within me to everyone I meet?

Rosary Prayer (One Decade)

Opening Prayer: Come Holy Spirit, Sweet Spouse of the Blessed Virgin Mary and Spouse of my soul. Purify and prepare my heart to be a virginal womb in which Divine Love may grow. May Jesus find His place of rest and delight here in the womb of my heart. Amen.

Apostles' Creed
Our Father
3 Hail Marys

Hail Mary full of grace, the Lord is with thee. Blessed art thou amongst women and blessed is the fruit of thy womb, Jesus. Holy Mary, Mother of God, **make my heart like unto thy virginal womb**, and pray for us sinners now and at the hour of our death. Amen.

Glory Be

The Second Joyful Mystery

The Visitation

Prayer: Awake north wind, come wind of the south! Breathe over the hidden garden of my heart and spread the sweet scent of Divine Love all around (see The Song of Songs 4:16). May the hearts you bring into my life recognize the fragrance of the Bridegroom dwelling within me just as at the Visitation, the babe in Elizabeth's womb recognized His hidden presence within the womb of the Blessed Mother. Amen.

> *"I come into my garden, my sister, my promised bride, I gather my myrrh and balsam, I eat my honey and my honeycomb, I drink my wine and my milk. Eat, friends, and drink, drink deep, my dearest friends." Song of Songs 5:1*

Our Father, 10 Hail Marys

Hail Mary full of grace, the Lord is with thee. Blessed art thou amongst women and blessed is the fruit of thy womb, Jesus. Holy Mary, Mother of God, **make my heart like unto thy virginal womb**, and pray for us sinners now and at the hour of our death. Amen.

Glory Be, Fatima Prayer

Closing Prayer:

Jesus, Sweet Spouse of my soul, I open the womb of my heart to You. Come and enter Your enclosed garden with the same incarnate love with which You entered the immaculate womb of Your Blessed Mother. In me, with me, and through me, bring the joy of Your Divine Love to birth again today. Amen.

The Nativity (1858)
Arthur Hughes (English, 1832 – 1915)

Day 4 - The Joyful Mysteries

The Third Joyful Mystery:
The Nativity of Jesus

Scripture: Luke 2:1-20

"Now it happened that at this time Caesar Augustus issued a decree that a census should be made of the whole inhabited world. This census - the first - took place while Quirinius was governor of Syria, and everyone went to be registered, each to his own town. So Joseph set out from the town of Nazareth in Galilee for Judaea, to David's town called Bethlehem, since he was of David's House and line, in order to be registered together with Mary, his betrothed, who was with child. Now it happened that, while they were there, the time came for her to have her child, and she gave birth to a son, her first-born. She wrapped him in swaddling clothes and laid him in a manger because there was no room for them in the living-space. In the countryside close by there were shepherds out in the fields keeping guard over their sheep during the watches of the night. An angel of the Lord stood over them

and the glory of the Lord shone round them. They were terrified, but the angel said, 'Do not be afraid. Look, I bring you news of great joy, a joy to be shared by the whole people. Today in the town of David a Saviour has been born to you; he is Christ the Lord. And here is a sign for you: you will find a baby wrapped in swaddling clothes and lying in a manger.' And all at once with the angel there was a great throng of the hosts of heaven, praising God with the words: Glory to God in the highest heaven, and on earth peace for those he favours. Now it happened that when the angels had gone from them into heaven, the shepherds said to one another, 'Let us go to Bethlehem and see this event which the Lord has made known to us.' So they hurried away and found Mary and Joseph, and the baby lying in the manger. When they saw the child they repeated what they had been told about him, and everyone who heard it was astonished at what the shepherds said to them. As for Mary, she treasured all these things and pondered them in her heart. And the shepherds went back glorifying and praising God for all they had heard and seen, just as they had been told."

Wisdom from the Saints

"A person is his bride when his faithful soul is united with Jesus Christ by the Holy Spirit; we are his brothers when we do the will of his Father who is in heaven (cf. Mt. 12: 50), and we are mothers to him when we enthrone him in our hearts and souls by love with a pure and sincere conscience, and give him birth by doing good." - St. Francis of Assisi

"God the Son wishes to form Himself, and, so to speak, to incarnate Himself, every day by His dear Mother in His members." - St. Louis de Montfort

"Our body is a cenacle, a monstrance: through its crystal the world should see God." - St. Gianna Molla

Reflection

In yesterday's reflection, we pondered the truth that each of us is a living tabernacle carrying the hidden Christ within us. Today, our focus shifts to the nativity of Christ. He is no longer hidden within

Mary's womb. Mary has given birth to Jesus, Emmanuel, God-With-Us, and the invisible God has become visible. The Heart of God cries with cold and hunger; the Love of God has a face and tiny hands that reach for His Mama. The birth of Jesus was a moment in salvation history, yet the birthing of His Love goes on throughout all of eternity. God invites you to become a living monstrance, a breathing temple, a life-giving womb. Christ wants to be born again in you. Being born in you, He can then be born through you into the world. This is the glory for which you were created.

Questions for Journaling and Reflection

- What emotions do you think Mother Mary felt as she was giving birth to Jesus? When she held Him in her arms and looked into His eyes for the first time? Talk to her about what this moment of seeing her God face to face was like.
- How do you give birth to Jesus "by doing good"?

- What does it mean to you to be both a living tabernacle and a living monstrance?
- Today's passage from the Song of Songs is the Bride's description of her Beloved to the daughters of Jerusalem. Spend a few moments with this passage and imagine Mother Mary introducing you to the Infant Bridegroom with these words of praise.

Rosary Prayer (One Decade)

Opening Prayer: Come Holy Spirit, Sweet Spouse of the Blessed Virgin Mary and Spouse of my soul. Purify and prepare my heart to be a virginal womb in which Divine Love may grow. May Jesus find His place of rest and delight here in the womb of my heart. Amen.

Apostles' Creed
Our Father
3 Hail Marys

Hail Mary full of grace, the Lord is with thee. Blessed art thou amongst women and blessed is the fruit of thy womb, Jesus. Holy Mary, Mother of God, **make my heart like unto thy virginal womb**, and pray for us sinners now and at the hour of our death. Amen.

Glory Be

The Third Joyful Mystery: The Nativity of Jesus

Prayer: Divine Love blossoming within the womb of my heart is not meant to remain hidden. May I en-flesh Love with my own body and may my life be a continual act of birthing Incarnate Love into this time and place. Mary, Mother and Bride, teach me how to spiritually give birth to Jesus again and again. Amen.

> *"My Beloved is fresh and ruddy, to be known
>   among ten thousand.*
> *His head is golden, purest gold, his locks are palm
>   fronds and black as the raven.*
> *His eyes are doves at a pool of water, bathed in
>   milk, at rest on a pool.*
> *His cheeks are beds of spices, banks sweetly scented.*
>   *His lips are lilies, distilling pure myrrh.*

*His hands are golden, rounded, set with jewels of
    Tarshish. His belly a block of ivory covered
    with sapphires.*

*His legs are alabaster columns set in sockets of pure
    gold. His appearance is that of Lebanon, unri-
    valled as the cedars.*

*His conversation is sweetness itself, he is altogether
    lovable. Such is my Beloved, such is my friend,
    O daughters of Jerusalem." Song of Songs 5:10-
    16*

Our Father, 10 Hail Marys

Hail Mary full of grace, the Lord is with thee. Blessed
art thou amongst women and blessed is the fruit of
thy womb, Jesus. Holy Mary, Mother of God, **make
my heart like unto thy virginal womb**, and pray for
us sinners now and at the hour of our death. Amen.

Glory Be, Fatima Prayer

Closing Prayer:

Jesus, Sweet Spouse of my soul, I open the womb of my heart to You. Come and enter Your enclosed garden with the same incarnate love with which You entered the immaculate womb of Your Blessed Mother. In me, with me, and through me, bring the joy of Your Divine Love to birth again today. Amen.

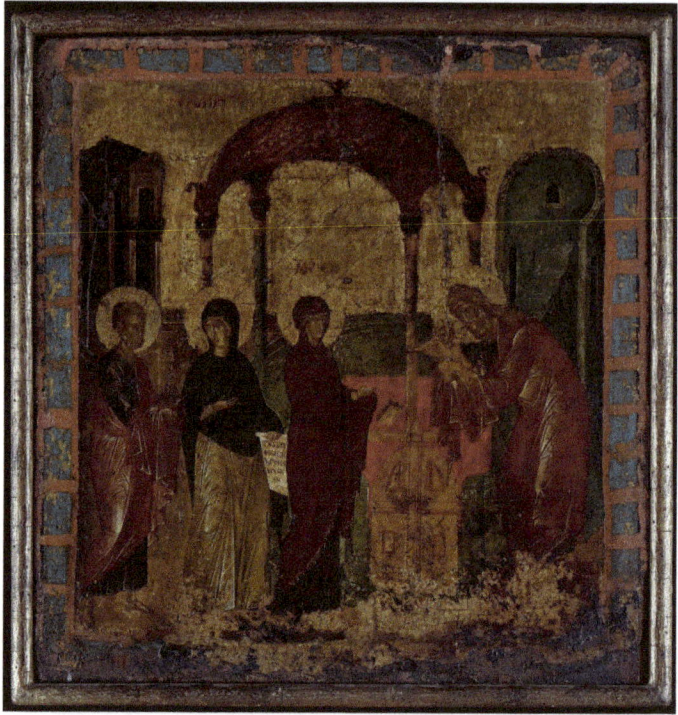

The Presentation in the Temple
Unknown Byzantine Painter

Day 5 - The Joyful Mysteries

The Fourth Joyful Mystery:
The Presentation of Jesus in the Temple

Scripture: Luke 2:22-40

"And when the day came for them to be purified in keeping with the Law of Moses, they took him up to Jerusalem to present him to the Lord- observing what is written in the Law of the Lord: Every first-born male must be consecrated to the Lord- and also to offer in sacrifice, in accordance with what is prescribed in the Law of the Lord, a pair of turtle-doves or two young pigeons. Now in Jerusalem there was a man named Simeon. He was an up-right and devout man; he looked forward to the restoration of Israel and the Holy Spirit rested on him. It had been revealed to him by the Holy Spirit that he would not see death until he had set eyes on the Christ of the Lord. Prompted by the Spirit he came to the Temple; and when the parents brought in the child Jesus to do for him what the Law required, he took him into his arms and

*blessed God; and he said: Now, Master, you are let-
ting your servant go in peace as you promised; for
my eyes have seen the salvation which you have
made ready in the sight of the nations; a light of
revelation for the gentiles and glory for your people
Israel. As the child's father and mother were won-
dering at the things that were being said about
him, Simeon blessed them and said to Mary his
mother, 'Look, he is destined for the fall and for the
rise of many in Israel, destined to be a sign that is
opposed- and a sword will pierce your soul too - so
that the secret thoughts of many may be laid bare.'
There was a prophetess, too, Anna the daughter of
Phanuel, of the tribe of Asher. She was well on in
years. Her days of girlhood over, she had been married for seven years before becoming a widow. She
was now eighty-four years old and never left the
Temple, serving God night and day with fasting
and prayer. She came up just at that moment and
began to praise God; and she spoke of the child to
all who looked forward to the deliverance of Jerusalem. When they had done everything the Law of
the Lord required, they went back to Galilee, to
their own town of Nazareth. And as the child grew
to maturity, he was filled with wisdom; and God's
favour was with him."*

Wisdom from the Saints

"Being a disciple means being constantly ready to bring the love of Jesus to others, and this can happen unexpectedly and in any place: on the street, in a city square, during work, on a journey." - Pope Francis

"The secret of everything is to let oneself be carried by God and so to carry Him to others." -St. John XXIII

"Jesus is living next to you, in the brothers and sisters with whom you share your daily existence." St. John Paul II

Reflection

Mary and Joseph climbed the steps of the temple in Jerusalem holding the baby Jesus in their arms. This was a royal procession, yet no one but Simeon and Anna recognized the King of Kings. His royalty and divinity were hidden within flesh and blood as in a "column of smoke"; "What is this coming up from the desert like a column of smoke, breathing of myrrh and frankincense and every perfume the merchant knows?" (Song of Songs 3:6).

The royal procession entered the Temple and Simeon and Anna accepted the long-awaited invitation to "come and see King Solomon" - Christ the new and true King of Peace. The diadem He wore is not the crown they expected their Messiah to come wearing, yet what a stunningly beautiful crown it was! For "the diadem with which his mother crowned him on his wedding day" (Song of Songs 3:11) is the crown of Sacred Humanity. On the wedding day of His Incarnation, within His mother's womb, His divinity married our humanity, and His heart leapt with joy. The Bridegroom has divinized our fallen humanity and our hearts are full of awe and thanksgiving. Let us rejoice with Simeon and Anna!

We need not travel back in time or to Israel to encounter the Bridegroom, for He comes to us veiled in the appearances of bread and wine. In every Holy Mass, we receive Him in His totality - His Sacred Humanity and His Divinity - but a humble, receptive heart is needed to "see" Him in such hiddenness. The faithful and perceptive spouse of Christ knows that each devoted reception of the Eucharist is a participation in the Eternal Wedding Feast of the Lamb, and we, His brides, become the royal throne, the living monstrance, that carries Christ into the world.

Now it is our turn to carry Jesus, hidden within the temples of our bodies, *"For we are the temple of the living God…" (2 Corinthians 6:16)*, and to present Him to all those whom we encounter. Their physical eyes cannot see His Presence but we reveal Him by our love. We become the "fragrance of Christ" (2 Corinthians 2:15), and like incense in the temple, our lives spread His perfume and draw souls to Him.

"Delicate is the fragrance of your perfume, your name is an oil poured out, and that is why the maidens love you." (Song of Songs 1:3)

Questions for Journaling and Reflection

- Can you recall a time when someone "presented" the love of Christ to you and you responded with joy and hope as Simeon did?
- Pray with 2 Corinthians 2:15. *"For we are a fragrance of Christ to God among those who*

are being saved and among those who are per-
ishing..."

- In the event of the Presentation in the Temple, Joseph and Mary were offering a sacrifice
  of praise and thanksgiving to God for the gift
  of Jesus. How can you offer a sacrifice of
  praise to the Father for the gift of Jesus?

Rosary Prayer (One Decade)

Opening Prayer: Come Holy Spirit, Sweet Spouse of
the Blessed Virgin Mary and Spouse of my soul. Purify and prepare my heart to be a virginal womb in
which Divine Love may grow. May Jesus find His
place of rest and delight here in the womb of my
heart. Amen.

Apostles' Creed
Our Father
3 Hail Marys

Hail Mary full of grace, the Lord is with thee. Blessed
art thou amongst women and blessed is the fruit of
thy womb, Jesus. Holy Mary, Mother of God, **make**

my heart like unto thy virginal womb, and pray for us sinners now and at the hour of our death. Amen.

Glory Be

The Fourth Joyful Mystery: The Presentation of Jesus in the Temple

Prayer: Come Holy Spirit, Sweet Spouse of the Blessed Virgin Mary and Spouse of my soul. Grant me the grace to present the Divine Love hidden in the womb of my heart with reverence and unshakeable faith to all whom You send to me. Give them the eyes of Simeon so they may exclaim, "my eyes have seen your salvation, your light, and your glory" (cf. Luke 2:30). Amen.

> "What is this coming up from the desert like a column of smoke, breathing of myrrh and frankincense and every perfume the merchant knows?
> See, it is the litter of Solomon. Around it are sixty champions, the flower of the warriors of Israel;

all of them skilled swordsmen, veterans of battle. Each man has his sword at his side, against alarms by night.

King Solomon has made himself a throne of wood from Lebanon.

The posts he has made of silver, the canopy of gold, the seat of purple; the back is inlaid with ebony.

Daughters of Zion, come and see King Solomon, wearing the diadem with which his mother crowned him on his wedding day, on the day of his heart's joy." (Song of Songs 3:6-11)

Our Father, 10 Hail Marys

Hail Mary full of grace, the Lord is with thee. Blessed art thou amongst women and blessed is the fruit of thy womb, Jesus. Holy Mary, Mother of God, **make my heart like unto thy virginal womb**, and pray for us sinners now and at the hour of our death. Amen.

Glory Be, Fatima Prayer

Closing Prayer:

Jesus, Sweet Spouse of my soul, I open the womb of my heart to You. Come and enter Your enclosed garden with the same incarnate love with which You entered the immaculate womb of Your Blessed Mother. In me, with me, and through me, bring the joy of Your Divine Love to birth again today. Amen.

Mary and Joseph Find
the Twelve-Year-Old Jesus in the Temple
(Artist Unknown)

Day 6 - The Joyful Mysteries

The Fifth Joyful Mystery:
Finding Jesus in the Temple

Scripture: Luke 2: 41-52

"Every year his parents used to go to Jerusalem for the feast of the Passover. When he was twelve years old, they went up for the feast as usual. When the days of the feast were over and they set off home, the boy Jesus stayed behind in Jerusalem without his parents knowing it. They assumed he was somewhere in the party, and it was only after a day's journey that they went to look for him among their relations and acquaintances. When they failed to find him they went back to Jerusalem looking for him everywhere. It happened that, three days later, they found him in the Temple, sitting among the teachers, listening to them, and asking them questions; and all those who heard him were astounded at his intelligence and his replies. They were overcome when they saw him, and his mother said to him, 'My child, why have you done this to us? See how worried your father and I

*have been, looking for you.' He replied, 'Why were
you looking for me? Did you not know that I must
be in my Father's house?' But they did not understand what he meant. He went down with them
then and came to Nazareth and lived under their
authority. His mother stored up all these things in
her heart. And Jesus increased in wisdom, in stat-
ure, and in favour with God and with people."*

Wisdom from the Saints

*"The child Jesus born within us advances by differ-
ent ways in those who receive him in wisdom, in
age and in grace." - St. Gregory of Nyssa*

"Seek Him, find Him, and keep Him." – St. Teresa
of Avila

Reflection

Seeking and finding God is a recurring theme
throughout Scripture and is especially prominent in
the Song of Songs. We, like the Bride of the Song and
Joseph and Mary in this Mystery of the Rosary, seek

the One Whom our souls love. The very act of seeking is already a grace, for God Himself has stirred the desire within us.

Joseph and Mary found Him after three days of searching. They found Him in the temple, sitting among the teachers, astonishing all with His wisdom (Luke 2:41–52). Their seeking was filled with worry, yet it led them to a deeper revelation of who He truly is. In the same way, our own seeking, even when it feels like struggle or absence, draws us into deeper knowledge of God's presence.

We often believe that we need dramatic signs in order to find Jesus. Or, like the Bride of the Song, we search for Him in all the wrong places. St. Augustine, St. John of the Cross, and St. Elizabeth of the Trinity remind us that the Bridegroom is to be found within the deepest center of our being. His presence is discovered in ordinary moments through prayer, reading His Word, contemplating the beauty of His creation, sharing His love with others. Seeking leads to finding, and finding deepens the desire to seek again, drawing us ever closer to the One who is the fulfillment of all longing. The more we seek Him, the more we discover that He is nearer than we imagined. He is Emmanuel, "God-with-us."

> *"You will seek me and find me; when you search for me with all your heart, I will let you find me, says the Lord."* Jeremiah 29:13–14

Questions for Journaling and Reflection

- Where do I feel I have 'lost' Jesus in my life?
- How do I actively seek Him each day?
- What joy do I find when I rediscover His presence?

Rosary Prayer (One Decade)

Opening Prayer: Come Holy Spirit, Sweet Spouse of the Blessed Virgin Mary and Spouse of my soul. Purify and prepare my heart to be a virginal womb in which Divine Love may grow. May Jesus find His place of rest and delight here in the womb of my heart. Amen.

Apostles' Creed
Our Father
3 Hail Marys

Hail Mary full of grace, the Lord is with thee. Blessed art thou amongst women and blessed is the fruit of thy womb, Jesus. Holy Mary, Mother of God, **make my heart like unto thy virginal womb**, and pray for us sinners now and at the hour of our death. Amen.

Glory Be

The Fifth Joyful Mystery: Finding Jesus in the Temple

Prayer: Mary, Mother and Bride, when I am crying out, "Have you seen the One Whom my heart loves? I sought Him but did not find Him!" (cf. Song of Songs 3:4), please gently remind me that my Beloved is always hidden in the womb of my heart. I need only return to silence and recollection, and I shall find Him doing His Father's work of loving and healing right here in my heart, a garden, a temple, and a womb, all for Him. Amen.

"On my bed, at night, I sought him whom my heart loves. I sought but did not find him. So I will rise and go through the City; in the streets and the squares I will seek him whom my heart loves. … I sought but did not find him. The watchmen came upon me on their rounds in the City: 'Have you seen him whom my heart loves?' Scarcely had I passed them then I found him whom my heart loves. I held him fast, nor would I let him go…" *(Song of Songs 3:1-4)*

Our Father, 10 Hail Marys

Hail Mary full of grace, the Lord is with thee. Blessed art thou amongst women and blessed is the fruit of thy womb, Jesus. Holy Mary, Mother of God, **make my heart like unto thy virginal womb**, and pray for us sinners now and at the hour of our death. Amen.

Glory Be, Fatima Prayer

Closing Prayer:

Jesus, Sweet Spouse of my soul, I open the womb of my heart to You. Come and enter Your enclosed garden with the same incarnate love with which You entered the immaculate womb of Your Blessed Mother. In me, with me, and through me, bring the joy of Your Divine Love to birth again today. Amen.

Day 7

Praying the Full
Joyful Mysteries of the Rosary

Reflection

In all the events we remember in the Joyful Mysteries, Mary receives. She receives the Word at the Annunciation, her cousin Elizabeth at the Visitation, the Christ Child at the Nativity, God's plan at the Presentation, and God's wisdom in the Finding in the Temple. She is the model of a receptive bride, receiving the love of her Divine Bridegroom in her heart and her body. Upon receiving the gift of the Bridegroom, she ponders and nurtures it. But it is not enough for the bride to receive the love her Bridegroom offers. Authentic love is total, free, faithful, and fruitful. Mary gives birth to Incarnate Love wrapped in her humanity in the Person of Jesus Christ. We are called to receive His love and spiritually birth Him again, enfleshed in our own lives.

May Mother Mary share with us the joy of surrendering to the will of God so we might be His fruitful brides.

Questions for Journaling and Reflection

- Which Joyful Mystery spoke most deeply to me this week?
- How am I cultivating a more receptive heart like Mary?
- Write your own prayer to Mother Mary inspired by this week's pondering of the Joyful Mysteries.

Praying the Rosary

The Joyful Mysteries

Opening Prayer: Come Holy Spirit, Sweet Spouse of the Blessed Virgin Mary and Spouse of my soul. Purify and prepare my heart to be a virginal womb in which Divine Love may grow. May Jesus find His place of rest and delight here in the womb of my heart. Amen.

Apostles' Creed
Our Father
3 Hail Marys

Hail Mary full of grace, the Lord is with thee. Blessed art thou amongst women and blessed is the fruit of thy womb, Jesus. Holy Mary, Mother of God, **make my heart like unto thy virginal womb**, and pray for us sinners now and at the hour of our death. Amen.

Glory Be

The First Joyful Mystery: The Annunciation

Prayer: Come Holy Spirit and plant the seeds of Divine Love in the womb of my heart. Water my Beloved's garden with honey-kissed dew drops of grace. May His love blossom and grow within me. Amen.
Our Father, 10 Hail Marys

Hail Mary full of grace, the Lord is with thee. Blessed art thou amongst women and blessed is the fruit of thy womb, Jesus. Holy Mary, Mother of God, **make**

my heart like unto thy virginal womb, and pray for us sinners now and at the hour of our death. Amen.

Glory Be, Fatima Prayer

The Second Joyful Mystery: The Visitation

Prayer: Awake north wind, come wind of the south! Breathe over the hidden garden of my heart and spread the sweet scent of Divine Love all around (see The Song of Songs 4:16). May the hearts you bring into my life recognize the fragrance of the Bridegroom dwelling within me just as at the Visitation, the babe in Elizabeth's womb recognized His hidden presence within the womb of the Blessed Mother. Amen.

Our Father, 10 Hail Marys

Hail Mary full of grace, the Lord is with thee. Blessed art thou amongst women and blessed is the fruit of thy womb, Jesus. Holy Mary, Mother of God, **make my heart like unto thy virginal womb,** and pray for us sinners now and at the hour of our death. Amen.

Glory Be, Fatima Prayer

The Third Joyful Mystery: The Nativity of Jesus

Prayer: Divine Love blossoming within the womb of my heart is not meant to remain hidden. May I enflesh Love with my own body and may my life be a continual act of birthing Incarnate Love into this time and place. Mary, Mother and Bride, teach me how to spiritually give birth to Jesus again and again. Amen.

Our Father, 10 Hail Marys

Hail Mary full of grace, the Lord is with thee. Blessed art thou amongst women and blessed is the fruit of thy womb, Jesus. Holy Mary, Mother of God, **make my heart like unto thy virginal womb**, and pray for us sinners now and at the hour of our death. Amen. Glory Be, Fatima Prayer

The Fourth Joyful Mystery: The Presentation of Jesus in the Temple

Prayer: Come Holy Spirit, Sweet Spouse of the Blessed Virgin Mary and Spouse of my soul. Grant me the grace to present the Divine Love hidden in the womb of my heart with reverence and unshakeable faith to all whom You send to me. Give them the eyes of Simeon so they may exclaim, "my eyes have seen your salvation, your light, and your glory" (cf. Luke 2:30). Amen.

Our Father, 10 Hail Marys

Hail Mary full of grace, the Lord is with thee. Blessed art thou amongst women and blessed is the fruit of thy womb, Jesus. Holy Mary, Mother of God, **make my heart like unto thy virginal womb**, and pray for us sinners now and at the hour of our death. Amen. Glory Be, Fatima Prayer

The Fifth Joyful Mystery: Finding Jesus in the Temple

Prayer: Mary, Mother and Bride, when I am crying out, "Have you seen the One Whom my heart loves? I sought Him but did not find Him!" (cf. Song of Songs 3:4), please gently remind me that my Beloved is always hidden in the womb of my heart. I need only return to silence and recollection, and I shall find Him doing His Father's work of loving and healing right here in my heart, a garden, a temple, and a womb, all for Him. Amen.

Our Father, 10 Hail Marys

Hail Mary full of grace, the Lord is with thee. Blessed art thou amongst women and blessed is the fruit of thy womb, Jesus. Holy Mary, Mother of God, **make my heart like unto thy virginal womb**, and pray for us sinners now and at the hour of our death. Amen.

Glory Be, Fatima Prayer

Closing Prayer:

Jesus, Sweet Spouse of my soul, I open the womb of my heart to You. Come and enter Your enclosed garden with the same incarnate love with which You entered the immaculate womb of Your Blessed Mother. In me, with me, and through me, bring the joy of Your Divine Love to birth again today. Amen.

Hail Holy Queen

The Luminous Mysteries

Jésus et Saint-Jean (étude pour 'Le baptême du Christ')
(ca 1844-1845)
Jean-Baptiste-Camille Corot (French, 1796 - 1875)

Day 8 - The Luminous Mysteries

The First Luminous Mystery:
The Baptism in the Jordan

Scripture: Matthew 3:13-17

"Then Jesus appeared: he came from Galilee to the Jordan to be baptised by John. John tried to dissuade him, with the words, 'It is I who need baptism from you, and yet you come to me!' But Jesus replied, 'Leave it like this for the time being; it is fitting that we should, in this way, do all that uprightness demands.' Then John gave in to him. And when Jesus had been baptised he at once came up from the water, and suddenly the heavens opened and he saw the Spirit of God descending like a dove and coming down on him. And suddenly there was a voice from heaven, 'This is my Son, the Beloved; my favour rests on him.'"

Wisdom from the Saints

"In Baptism we are sealed with the indelible spiritual mark of belonging to Christ." - St. John Paul II

"Our souls are imprinted with a character that marks us as God's own." - St. Augustine

"Baptism is seen in its fullness as a nuptial mystery. The soul, until now a simple creature, becomes the Bride of Christ. When she comes out of the baptismal water in which He has purified her in His Blood, He welcomes her in her white bridal robe and receives the promise which binds her to Him forever." -Jean Daniélou

Reflection

As we ponder Jesus' baptism in the Jordan River, we remember that Blessed Mary, conceived without sin, did not need the Sacrament of Baptism to prepare her soul for union with God. For His part, Christ certainly did not consent to be baptized by St. John the Baptist out of a need for repentance. He descended into the waters not to be cleansed, but to sanctify the waters themselves and to provide a model for us. As the waters of the Jordan River flowed over Jesus, the voice of the Father was heard, "This is My beloved Son with whom I am well pleased" (Matthew 3:17). Similarly, as the waters of Baptism flowed over each of us, the Father spoke these same words. He continues to speak and sing His love over us in every moment. Living in our baptismal identity means being rooted in the truth of our belovedness. Only a heart confident in God's unconditional love will feel safe enough to become an open and available womb for Him. Mary had such confidence and fearless trust in her identity as God's beloved, and so she was able to give her consent to His will.

Questions for Journaling and Reflection

- Do I truly believe that I am the Father's beloved son or daughter?
- How does my baptism shape the way I live my daily life?
- Where am I being invited to live more fully in my baptismal dignity?

Rosary Prayer (One Decade)

Opening Prayer: Come Holy Spirit, Sweet Spouse of the Blessed Virgin Mary and Spouse of my soul. Purify and prepare my heart to be a virginal womb in which Divine Love may grow. May Jesus find His place of rest and delight here in the womb of my heart. Amen.

Apostles' Creed
Our Father
3 Hail Marys

Hail Mary full of grace, the Lord is with thee. Blessed art thou amongst women and blessed is the fruit of thy womb, Jesus. Holy Mary, Mother of God, **make my heart like unto thy virginal womb**, and pray for us sinners now and at the hour of our death. Amen.

Glory Be

The First Luminous Mystery: The Baptism in the Jordan

Prayer: Open the womb of my heart to Your Holy Spirit. Cleanse and purify my heart and make it like unto Mary's virginal womb so by the power of Your Spirit, I too, may conceive Your love. Let it be done unto me according to Your Word.

"Set me like a seal on your heart, like a seal on your arm. For love is strong as Death, jealousy relentless as Sheol. The flash of it is a flash of fire, a flame of Yahweh himself. Love no flood can quench, no torrents drown." (Song of Songs 8:6-7)

Our Father, 10 Hail Marys

Hail Mary full of grace, the Lord is with thee. Blessed art thou amongst women and blessed is the fruit of thy womb, Jesus. Holy Mary, Mother of God, **make my heart like unto thy virginal womb**, and pray for us sinners now and at the hour of our death. Amen.

Glory Be, Fatima Prayer

Closing Prayer:

Jesus, Sweet Spouse of my soul, I open the womb of my heart to You. Come and enter Your enclosed garden with the same incarnate love with which You entered the immaculate womb of Your Blessed Mother. In me, with me, and through me, bring the joy of Your Divine Love to birth again today. Amen.

Queen Mary Psalter Marriage feast at Cana
British Museum image, ca. 1320

Day 9 - The Luminous Mysteries

The Second Luminous Mystery:
The Miracle at the Wedding Feast in Cana

Scripture: John 2: 1-11

"On the third day there was a wedding at Cana in Galilee. The mother of Jesus was there, and Jesus and his disciples had also been invited. And they ran out of wine, since the wine provided for the feast had all been used, and the mother of Jesus said to him, 'They have no wine.' Jesus said, 'Woman, what do you want from me? My hour has not come yet.' His mother said to the servants, 'Do whatever he tells you.' There were six stone water jars standing there, meant for the ablutions that are customary among the Jews: each could hold twenty or thirty gallons. Jesus said to the servants, 'Fill the jars with water,' and they filled them to the brim. Then he said to them, 'Draw some out now and take it to the president of the feast.' They did this; the president tasted the water, and it had turned into wine. Having no idea where it came

from - though the servants who had drawn the water knew - the president of the feast called the bridegroom and said, 'Everyone serves good wine first and the worse wine when the guests are well wined; but you have kept the best wine till now.' This was the first of Jesus' signs: it was at Cana in Galilee. He revealed his glory, and his disciples believed in him."

Wisdom from the Saints

"Mary is the surest, the easiest, the shortest and the most perfect means of going to Jesus Christ." - St. Louis de Montfort

"To succeed in your intentions, entrust yourselves to the Blessed Virgin Mary always, but especially in moments of difficulty and darkness. From Mary we learn to surrender to God's will in things. From Mary we learn to trust even when all hope seems gone. From Mary we learn to love Christ, her Son and the Son of God…Learn from her to be always faithful, to trust that God's Word to you will be fulfilled, and that nothing is impossible with God." - St. John Paul II

"Let us run to Mary, and, as her little children, cast ourselves into her arms with a perfect confidence."
- Saint Francis de Sales

Reflection

As we ponder the emptiness of the wine vessels at this wedding feast, we are reminded of the emptiness, the availability of Mary's hands, heart, and womb on that day thirty years prior when the angel Gabriel came to her. In the miracle of the Annunciation, as well as this miracle at Cana, Mary is not ashamed of emptiness, of lack, of need. Her humility and fearless trust in the goodness and power of God allow her to see emptiness as an opportunity for encounter with Him Who is Fullness. Her life with God has taught her that emptiness, offered to Him, leads to miracles of abundance - abundant life and overflowing love.

Mary, conceived without sin, is the perfect Bride who knows and believes that God, the Divine Bridegroom, is the fulfillment of all her desires and the only One with the power to provide for all her needs. Just as at Cana when she sent the servants to the true

Bridegroom, so she always leads us to Christ and re-minds us to do whatever He tells us.

Questions for Journaling and Reflection

- What do I need to let go of so that the womb of my heart will be more available to the Bridegroom?
- How can I listen more attentively to Mary's maternal guidance?
- What 'ordinary water' in my life might Christ want to transform into 'new wine'?

Rosary Prayer (One Decade)

Opening Prayer: Come Holy Spirit, Sweet Spouse of the Blessed Virgin Mary and Spouse of my soul. Purify and prepare my heart to be a virginal womb in which Divine Love may grow. May Jesus find His place of rest and delight here in the womb of my heart. Amen.

Apostles' Creed
Our Father

3 Hail Marys

Hail Mary full of grace, the Lord is with thee. Blessed art thou amongst women and blessed is the fruit of thy womb, Jesus. Holy Mary, Mother of God, **make my heart like unto thy virginal womb**, and pray for us sinners now and at the hour of our death. Amen.

Glory Be

The Second Luminous Mystery: The Miracle at the Wedding Feast in Cana

Prayer: Make new wine skin of my heart and transform the stagnant water of my tears and imperfections into the wine of Your joy and peace. Help me to let go of whatever takes up room in my heart so that You can fill me to overflowing with Your love. Pour Your new wine out into the world through me. *"The King has brought me into his rooms; you will be our joy and our gladness. We shall praise your love above wine; how right it is to love you." (Song of Songs 1:4)*

Our Father, 10 Hail Marys

Hail Mary full of grace, the Lord is with thee. Blessed art thou amongst women and blessed is the fruit of thy womb, Jesus. Holy Mary, Mother of God, **make my heart like unto thy virginal womb**, and pray for us sinners now and at the hour of our death. Amen. Glory Be, Fatima Prayer

Closing Prayer:

Jesus, Sweet Spouse of my soul, I open the womb of my heart to You. Come and enter Your enclosed garden with the same incarnate love with which You entered the immaculate womb of Your Blessed Mother. In me, with me, and through me, bring the joy of Your Divine Love to birth again today. Amen.

The Sermon on the Mount (1877)
Carl Block (1834-1890)

Day 10 - The Luminous Mysteries

The Third Luminous Mystery:
The Proclamation of the Kingdom
and His Call to Conversion

**Scripture: Mark 1:14-15, Romans 14:17,
Luke 17:20-21**

"After John had been arrested, Jesus went into Galilee. There he proclaimed the gospel from God saying, 'The time is fulfilled, and the kingdom of God is close at hand. Repent, and believe the gospel.'"

"The kingdom of God is not coming with things that can be observed; nor will they say, 'Look, here it is!' or 'There it is!' For, in fact, the kingdom of God is within you."

"The kingdom of God is not a matter of food and drink, but of righteousness, peace, and joy in the Holy Spirit."

Wisdom from the Saints

"If you are what you should be, you will set the whole world ablaze!" - St. Catherine of Siena

"Espousing the divine will for salvation whole-heartedly, without a single sin to restrain her, she gave herself entirely to the person and to the work of her Son; she did so in order to serve the mystery of redemption with him and dependent on him, by God's grace." CCC 494

Reflection:

The Bridegroom proclaims the Kingdom not as an idea, but as a living reality breaking into our world, being built within our hearts. His invitation is spousal: turn away from worldly affections and attachments, away from sin, and turn toward Love. Mary proclaimed the Kingdom of God with every fiber of her being! Within her heart and within her womb the King of the Kingdom of God dwelt - Body and Soul.

As we continue to pray that our hearts would be like unto Mary's virginal womb, we are giving the

King of Kings permission to build His Kingdom within us. Mary will teach us how to proclaim the coming of His Kingdom by our humble obedience and trust in the Father's will.

Questions for Journaling and Reflection

- Do I proclaim the Kingdom of God as Mary did?
- How do I live as a witness of God's Kingdom each day?
- What would it look like for Christ to reign more fully in me?

Rosary Prayer (One Decade)

Opening Prayer:

Come Holy Spirit, Sweet Spouse of the Blessed Virgin Mary and Spouse of my soul. Purify and prepare my heart to be a virginal womb in which Divine Love may grow. May Jesus find His place of rest and delight here in the womb of my heart. Amen.

Apostles' Creed
Our Father
3 Hail Marys

Hail Mary full of grace, the Lord is with thee. Blessed art thou amongst women and blessed is the fruit of thy womb, Jesus. Holy Mary, Mother of God, **make my heart like unto thy virginal womb**, and pray for us sinners now and at the hour of our death. Amen.

Glory Be

The Third Luminous Mystery: The Proclamation of the Kingdom and His Call to Conversion

Prayer: Till and prepare the soil of my heart making it fertile ground for the seed of Your Word. May my life proclaim the glory of Your Kingdom and give birth to the culture of love.

"You who dwell in the gardens, my companions listen for your voice; deign to let me hear it." Song of Songs 8:13

Our Father, 10 Hail Marys

Hail Mary full of grace, the Lord is with thee. Blessed art thou amongst women and blessed is the fruit of thy womb, Jesus. Holy Mary, Mother of God, **make my heart like unto thy virginal womb**, and pray for us sinners now and at the hour of our death. Amen.

Glory Be, Fatima Prayer

Closing Prayer:

Jesus, Sweet Spouse of my soul, I open the womb of my heart to You. Come and enter Your enclosed garden with the same incarnate love with which You entered the immaculate womb of Your Blessed Mother. In me, with me, and through me, bring the joy of Your Divine Love to birth again today. Amen.

Transfiguration of Jesus (1872)
Carl Bloch (Danish, 1834-1890)

Day 11 - The Luminous Mysteries

The Fourth Luminous Mystery: His Transfiguration

Scripture: Matthew 17:1-8

"Six days later, Jesus took with him Peter and James and his brother John and led them up a high mountain by themselves. There in their presence he was transfigured: his face shone like the sun and his clothes became as dazzling as light. And suddenly Moses and Elijah appeared to them; they were talking with him. Then Peter spoke to Jesus. 'Lord,' he said, 'it is wonderful for us to be here; if you want me to, I will make three shelters here, one for you, one for Moses and one for Elijah.' He was still speaking when suddenly a bright cloud covered them with shadow, and suddenly from the cloud there came a voice which said, 'This is my Son, the Beloved; he enjoys my favour. Listen to him.' When they heard this, the disciples fell on their faces, overcome with fear. But Jesus came up and touched them, saying, 'Stand up, do not be afraid.'

And when they raised their eyes they saw no one but Jesus."

Wisdom from the Saints

"Jesus took Peter, James, and John up a high mountain to show them the glory of His divinity."
- St. Thomas Aquinas

"The Transfiguration reveals the glory that awaits us if we remain faithful to Christ." - St. John Paul II

Reflection

On Mount Tabor, the Bridegroom unveils His divine beauty. The disciples are gifted with a revelation of Christ's glory, the glory that will one day be ours, too. "Our Lord Jesus Christ, through His transcendent love, became what we are, that He might bring us to be even what He is Himself" (St. Irenaus). This vision of Christ in His divinity gave hope and strength to the disciples as they witnessed the sufferings of Jesus. Pondering the Transfiguration of the Lord renews our hope as we continue the arduous journey through this valley of tears. It is important to remember that we do not travel alone. Even when the path is shrouded in darkness and our way becomes uncertain, the light of Christ remains with us. As we spend time in the presence of our radiant Bridegroom, the darkness in our hearts, our homes, and our world begin to dissipate as His pure light shines forth. May Mary, Mother Most Pure, Bearer of the Light, pray for us and help us to be unafraid of His piercing purifying Light. May Christ, the Light of the world, shine brightly from within the womb of our hearts.

"What has come into being in him was life, and the life was the light of all people. The light shines in the darkness, and the darkness did not overcome it." John 1:4-5

Questions for Journaling and Reflection

- Where do I see glimpses of God's glory breaking into my life?
- How can I 'listen to him' more attentively?
- What areas of darkness in me need the light of the Transfigured Christ?

- Write your own prayer asking Mother Mary to be your teacher as you learn to bear the light of Christ into the world.

Rosary Prayer (One Decade)

Opening Prayer:

Come Holy Spirit, Sweet Spouse of the Blessed Virgin Mary and Spouse of my soul. Purify and prepare my heart to be a virginal womb in which Divine Love may grow. May Jesus find His place of rest and delight here in the womb of my heart. Amen.

Apostles' Creed
Our Father
3 Hail Marys

Hail Mary full of grace, the Lord is with thee. Blessed art thou amongst women and blessed is the fruit of thy womb, Jesus. Holy Mary, Mother of God, **make my heart like unto thy virginal womb**, and pray for us sinners now and at the hour of our death. Amen.

Glory Be

The Fourth Luminous Mystery: The Transfiguration of Jesus

Prayer: On the Mount of Tabor, Peter, James, and John saw Your glory and radiance with unveiled eyes. This glimpse of Your light and divinity gave them hope and comfort in the days of darkness that were to come. Transform my heart with Your glory and radiance so I might shine Your light into the darkness and give others the hope and comfort You have given me.

> "'Who is this arising like the dawn, fair as the moon, resplendent as the sun, terrible as an army with banners?'" *Song of Songs* 6:10

Our Father, 10 Hail Marys

Hail Mary full of grace, the Lord is with thee. Blessed art thou amongst women and blessed is the fruit of thy womb, Jesus. Holy Mary, Mother of God, **make**

my heart like unto thy virginal womb, and pray for us sinners now and at the hour of our death. Amen.

Glory Be, Fatima Prayer

Closing Prayer:

Jesus, Sweet Spouse of my soul, I open the womb of my heart to You. Come and enter Your enclosed garden with the same incarnate love with which You entered the immaculate womb of Your Blessed Mother. In me, with me, and through me, bring the joy of Your Divine Love to birth again today. Amen.

Allegory of the Eucharist (Ca. 1676-1725)
Artist Unknown

Day 12 - The Luminous Mysteries

The Fifth Luminous Mystery:
The Institution of the Eucharist

Scripture: Luke 22: 14-20

"When the time came he took his place at table, and the apostles with him. And he said to them, 'I have ardently longed to eat this Passover with you before I suffer; because, I tell you, I shall not eat it until it is fulfilled in the kingdom of God.' Then, taking a cup, he gave thanks and said, 'Take this and share it among you, because from now on, I tell you, I shall never again drink wine until the kingdom of God comes.' Then he took bread, and when he had given thanks, he broke it and gave it to them, saying, 'This is my body given for you; do this in remembrance of me.' He did the same with the cup after supper, and said, 'This cup is the new covenant in my blood poured out for you."

Wisdom from the Saints

"The Eucharist is the consummation of the whole spiritual life." - St. Thomas Aquinas

"Jesus has prepared not just a banquet, but a wedding feast - Himself as the Bridegroom giving Himself to us." - St. John Paul II

Reflection

In the Eucharist, the Bridegroom gives Himself entirely, Body, Blood, Soul, and Divinity. The Eucharist is the wedding banquet of heaven and earth; it is the sacrament of the Bridegroom and the Bride. The Blessed Mother is present at every Holy Mass. She stands beside the priest at the altar as the Holy Spirit descends like the dewfall and Jesus becomes Incarnate once again. Wherever our Lord is enfleshed, His mother from whom He received His flesh, is present. In the Holy Eucharist, the same Incarnate Love which filled the Immaculate Womb of Blessed Mary now comes to fill the womb of our hearts. May He purify our hearts to be like unto Mary's Immaculate

Womb so we will be worthy dwelling places for our Lord.

Questions for Journaling and Reflection

- How do I prepare my heart to receive the Eucharist worthily?
- What does it mean to me that Christ gives Himself to me as my Bridegroom in the Sacrament of the Eucharist?
- How can I enflesh the Incarnate Love present in the Holy Eucharist?

Rosary Prayer (One Decade)

Opening Prayer:

Come Holy Spirit, Sweet Spouse of the Blessed Virgin Mary and Spouse of my soul. Purify and prepare my heart to be a virginal womb in which Divine Love may grow. May Jesus find His place of rest and delight here in the womb of my heart. Amen.

Apostles' Creed

Our Father

3 Hail Marys

Hail Mary full of grace, the Lord is with thee. Blessed art thou amongst women and blessed is the fruit of thy womb, Jesus. Holy Mary, Mother of God, **make my heart like unto thy virginal womb**, and pray for us sinners now and at the hour of our death. Amen.

Glory Be

The Fifth Luminous Mystery: The Institution and the Gift of the Eucharist

Prayer: In the bridal chamber of Mary's virginal womb, Your divinity wedded humanity, and she became the Mother of God and the Mother of the Eucharist. Fill my heart with the same incarnate love with which You filled the womb of Your Blessed Mother, and into which you transformed mere bread and wine. May I enflesh Your love, here and now, for the life of the world.

"Your navel is a bowl well rounded with no lack of wine, your belly a heap of wheat surrounded with lilies." Song of Songs 7:3

Our Father, 10 Hail Marys

Hail Mary full of grace, the Lord is with thee. Blessed art thou amongst women and blessed is the fruit of thy womb, Jesus. Holy Mary, Mother of God, **make my heart like unto thy virginal womb**, and pray for us sinners now and at the hour of our death. Amen.

Glory Be, Fatima Prayer

Closing Prayer:

Jesus, Sweet Spouse of my soul, I open the womb of my heart to You. Come and enter Your enclosed garden with the same incarnate love with which You entered the immaculate womb of Your Blessed Mother. In me, with me, and through me, bring the joy of Your Divine Love to birth again today. Amen.

Day 13 - Praying the Full Luminous Mysteries of the Rosary

Scripture

At the birth of John the Baptist, his father Zechariah proclaimed:

"And you, my child, will be called a prophet of the
Most High;

for you will go on before the Lord to prepare the
way for him,

to give his people the knowledge of salvation

through the forgiveness of their sins,

because of the tender mercy of our God,

by which the rising sun will come to us from
heaven

to shine on those living in darkness

and in the shadow of death,

to guide our feet into the path of peace."

~Luke 1:76-79

Reflection

In the events we meditate on in the Luminous Mysteries, Christ, the Light of the World, is revealed to His followers: as Beloved Son in the Jordan, as divine Bridegroom at Cana, as King proclaiming His Kingdom, as radiant Lord on Mt. Tabor, and as Eucharistic Bridegroom in the Upper Room. As we reflect on this moment in time when the veil between heaven and earth was lifted and the glory of God was revealed to men, let us ask our Blessed Mother to teach us reverence and awe for her Son, our King and Bridegroom. May we gaze upon His Beauty and allow His light to permeate our very beings so we, too, might be bearers of the Light of the world.

Questions for Journaling and Reflection

- Which Luminous Mystery most opened my eyes to the glory and beauty of Christ this week?
- How do I see Christ revealing Himself as the Bridegroom of my soul?

- In what ways is Mary guiding me as I grow in my desire to birth the light and love of Christ anew?

Praying the Rosary

The Luminous Mysteries

Opening Prayer:

Come Holy Spirit, Sweet Spouse of the Blessed Virgin Mary and Spouse of my soul. Purify and prepare my heart to be a virginal womb in which Divine Love may grow. May Jesus find His place of rest and delight here in the womb of my heart. Amen.

Apostles' Creed
Our Father
3 Hail Marys

Hail Mary full of grace, the Lord is with thee. Blessed art thou amongst women and blessed is the fruit of thy womb, Jesus. Holy Mary, Mother of God, **make**

my heart like unto thy virginal womb, and pray for us sinners now and at the hour of our death. Amen.

Glory Be

The First Luminous Mystery: The Baptism of Jesus in the Jordan

Prayer: Open the womb of my heart to Your Holy Spirit. Cleanse and purify my heart and make it like unto Mary's virginal womb so by the power of Your Spirit, I too, may conceive Your love. Let it be done unto me according to Your Word.

Our Father, 10 Hail Marys

Hail Mary full of grace, the Lord is with thee. Blessed art thou amongst women and blessed is the fruit of thy womb, Jesus. Holy Mary, Mother of God, **make my heart like unto thy virginal womb**, and pray for us sinners now and at the hour of our death. Amen.

Glory Be, Fatima Prayer

The Second Luminous Mystery: The Miracle at the Wedding Feast in Cana

Prayer: Make new wine skin of my heart and transform the stagnant water of my tears and imperfections into the wine of Your joy and peace. Fill me to overflowing and pour Your new wine out into the world.

Our Father, 10 Hail Marys

Hail Mary full of grace, the Lord is with thee. Blessed art thou amongst women and blessed is the fruit of thy womb, Jesus. Holy Mary, Mother of God, **make my heart like unto thy virginal womb**, and pray for us sinners now and at the hour of our death. Amen. Glory Be, Fatima Prayer

The Third Luminous Mystery: The Proclamation of the Kingdom and His Call to Conversion

Prayer: Till and prepare the soil of my heart making it fertile ground for the seed of Your Word. May my life proclaim the glory of Your Kingdom and give birth to the culture of love.

Our Father, 10 Hail Marys

Hail Mary full of grace, the Lord is with thee. Blessed art thou amongst women and blessed is the fruit of thy womb, Jesus. Holy Mary, Mother of God, **make my heart like unto thy virginal womb**, and pray for us sinners now and at the hour of our death. Amen. Glory Be, Fatima Prayer

The Fourth Luminous Mystery: His Transfiguration

Prayer: On the Mount of Tabor, Peter, James, and John saw Your glory and radiance with unveiled eyes. This glimpse of Your light and divinity gave them hope and comfort in the days of darkness that were to come. Transform my heart with Your glory and radiance so I might shine Your light into the darkness and give others the hope and comfort You have given me.

Our Father, 10 Hail Marys

Hail Mary full of grace, the Lord is with thee. Blessed art thou amongst women and blessed is the fruit of thy womb, Jesus. Holy Mary, Mother of God, **make my heart like unto thy virginal womb**, and pray for us sinners now and at the hour of our death. Amen. Glory Be, Fatima Prayer

The Fifth Luminous Mystery: The Institution and the Gift of the Eucharist

Prayer: IIn the bridal chamber of Mary's virginal womb, Your divinity wedded humanity, and she became the Mother of God and the Mother of the Eucharist. Fill my heart with the same incarnate love with which You filled the womb of Your Blessed Mother, and into which you transformed mere bread and wine. May I enflesh Your love, here and now, for the life of the world.

Our Father, 10 Hail Marys

Hail Mary full of grace, the Lord is with thee. Blessed art thou amongst women and blessed is the fruit of thy womb, Jesus. Holy Mary, Mother of God, **make my heart like unto thy virginal womb**, and pray for us sinners now and at the hour of our death. Amen.

Glory Be, Fatima Prayer

Closing Prayer:

Jesus, Sweet Spouse of my soul, I open the womb of my heart to You. Come and enter Your enclosed garden with the same incarnate love with which You entered the immaculate womb of Your Blessed Mother. In me, with me, and through me, bring the joy of Your Divine Love to birth again today. Amen.

Hail Holy Queen

The Sorrowful Mysteries

Agony in the Garden (1898)
Frans Schwartz (1850-1917)

Day 14 - The Sorrowful Mysteries

The First Sorrowful Mystery:
The Agony in the Garden

Scripture: Luke 22: 39-46

"He then left to make his way as usual to the Mount of Olives, with the disciples following. When he reached the place he said to them, 'Pray not to be put to the test.' Then he withdrew from them, about a stone's throw away, and knelt down and prayed. 'Father,' he said, 'if you are willing, take this cup away from me. Nevertheless, let your will be done, not mine.' Then an angel appeared to him, coming from heaven to give him strength. In his anguish he prayed even more earnestly, and his sweat fell to the ground like great drops of blood. When he rose from prayer he went to the disciples and found them sleeping for sheer grief. And he said to them, 'Why are you asleep? Get up and pray not to be put to the test.'"

Wisdom from the Saints

"Jesus, in the Garden of Olives, saw all our sins and, in spite of this, He took them all upon Himself." - St. John Vianney

"The will of God will never take you where the grace of God cannot sustain you." - St. Bernard of Clairvaux

Reflection

Today, we enter into the Sorrowful Mysteries of the Rosary and accompany Jesus and Mary in their suffering. Just as laboring to bring a new baby into the world is a painful process, Jesus and Mary endured tribulation and agony to birth our redemption and to make possible our reconciliation with God. As we continue to ask Mother Mary to make our hearts like unto her virginal womb, we need to ponder the truth that while the womb was created to nurture life, giving birth to that life requires pain and sacrifice. So too, Mary's heart had to be pierced by swords of sorrow; the Bridegroom had to be scourged and crucified so that we might have new life in Him.

Questions for Journaling and Reflection

- Where is God asking me to surrender my will to His?
- How do I respond to suffering and trial, with resistance or with trust?
- What consolation can I draw from Christ's willingness to suffer for me and with me?
- Reflect on seasons of your life when your suffering was the labor pains that gave birth to something new and beautiful.

Rosary Prayer (One Decade)

Opening Prayer:

Come Holy Spirit, Sweet Spouse of the Blessed Virgin Mary and Spouse of my soul. Purify and prepare my heart to be a virginal womb in which Divine Love may grow. May Jesus find His place of rest and delight here in the womb of my heart. Amen.

Apostles' Creed
Our Father

3 Hail Marys

Hail Mary full of grace, the Lord is with thee. Blessed art thou amongst women and blessed is the fruit of thy womb, Jesus. Holy Mary, Mother of God, **make my heart like unto thy virginal womb**, and pray for us sinners now and at the hour of our death. Amen.

Glory Be

The First Sorrowful Mystery: The Agony in the Garden

Prayer: Sorrowful Mother, pray for me and teach me fearless trust in the will of God. May I comfort Jesus in His agony by allowing my heart to be conformed to your Immaculate Heart so as to be a place of rest for Him. May the Father's will and not mine be done. *"I hear my Beloved knocking. 'Open to me, my sister, my love, my dove, my perfect one, for my head is covered with dew, my locks with the drops of night.'" Song of Songs 5:2*

Our Father, 10 Hail Marys

Hail Mary full of grace, the Lord is with thee. Blessed art thou amongst women and blessed is the fruit of thy womb, Jesus. Holy Mary, Mother of God, **make my heart like unto thy virginal womb**, and pray for us sinners now and at the hour of our death. Amen.

Glory Be, Fatima Prayer

Closing Prayer:

Jesus, Sweet Spouse of my soul, I open the womb of my heart to You. Come and enter Your enclosed garden with the same incarnate love with which You entered the immaculate womb of Your Blessed Mother. In me, with me, and through me, bring the joy of Your Divine Love to birth again today. Amen.

The Flagellation of Our Lord Jesus Christ (1880)
William Bouguereau (French, 1825-1905)

Day 15 - The Sorrowful Mysteries
The Second Sorrowful Mystery:
The Scourging at the Pillar

Scripture: John 19: 1-3

> *"Pilate then had Jesus taken away and scourged;*
> *and after this, the soldiers twisted some thorns into*
> *a crown and put it on his head and dressed him in*
> *a purple robe. They kept coming up to him and*
> *saying, 'Hail, king of the Jews!' and slapping him in*
> *the face."*

Wisdom from the Saints

> *"Jesus Christ bore our sins in His body on the tree,*
> *so that we might die to sins and live for righteous-*
> *ness; by His wounds you have been healed."*
> *- St. Peter (1 Peter 2:24)*

> *"The secret of His heart is laid open through the*
> *clefts of His body. That great mystery of love is re-*
> *vealed, those tender mercies of our God in which*
> *the Orient from on high has visited us. How could*

you show more clearly than by your wounds that
you, Lord, are indeed sweet and gentle, and full of
mercy?" - St. Bernard of Clairvaux, commentary of
verse 2:14 of the Song of Songs

Reflection

Christ's scourging reveals the cost of spousal love, a love that is free, total, faithful, and fruitful. The Bridegroom is beaten so His Bride may be healed - "He was wounded for our transgressions, crushed for our iniquities; upon him was the punishment that made us whole, and by his bruises we are healed" (Isaiah 53:5). Each lash proclaims His mercy poured out for us. Just as a mother's desire to hold her newborn child causes her to willingly suffer the pains of childbirth, His desire for us causes Him to willingly accept the torture and humiliation of the scourging. Jesus invites us to enter into the mystery of the agony and the ecstasy, the intertwining of pain and joy, death and life. May Mother Mary help us to ponder this mystery with gratitude, knowing His Wounds open the way to our healing and eternal happiness.

Questions for Journaling and Reflection

- What wounds in me still need Christ's healing?
- How do I see his mercy at work in my life?
- How can I be an instrument of healing love for others?

Rosary Prayer (One Decade)

Opening Prayer:

Come Holy Spirit, Sweet Spouse of the Blessed Virgin Mary and Spouse of my soul. Purify and prepare my heart to be a virginal womb in which Divine Love may grow. May Jesus find His place of rest and delight here in the womb of my heart. Amen.

Apostles' Creed

Our Father

3 Hail Marys

Hail Mary full of grace, the Lord is with thee. Blessed art thou amongst women and blessed is the fruit of thy womb, Jesus. Holy Mary, Mother of God, **make**

my heart like unto thy virginal womb, and pray for us sinners now and at the hour of our death. Amen.

Glory Be

The Second Sorrowful Mystery: The Scourging at the Pillar

Prayer: Sorrowful Mother, together let us hold and anoint the beaten Body of our Beloved Jesus. May my loving attentiveness to Him in His time of excruciating suffering be a soothing balm. And from Him, may I learn to accept that joy and sorrow will always be intertwined until the day He carries me over the threshold of the Father's house.

> *"My dove, hiding in the clefts of the rock, in the coverts of the cliff, show me your face, let me hear your voice; for your voice is sweet and your face is beautiful."* Song of Songs 2:14

Our Father, 10 Hail Marys

Hail Mary full of grace, the Lord is with thee. Blessed art thou amongst women and blessed is the fruit of thy womb, Jesus. Holy Mary, Mother of God, **make my heart like unto thy virginal womb**, and pray for us sinners now and at the hour of our death. Amen. Glory Be, Fatima Prayer

Closing Prayer:

Jesus, Sweet Spouse of my soul, I open the womb of my heart to You. Come and enter Your enclosed garden with the same incarnate love with which You entered the immaculate womb of Your Blessed Mother. In me, with me, and through me, bring the joy of Your Divine Love to birth again today. Amen.

The Crowning with Thorns (between 1602 and 1604)
Caravaggio (Italian, 1571-1610)

Day 16 - The Sorrowful Mysteries
The Third Sorrowful Mystery:
The Crowning with Thorns

Scripture: John 19: 2-3, Song of Songs 3:11

"And after this, the soldiers twisted some thorns into a crown and put it on his head and dressed him in a purple robe. They kept coming up to him and saying, 'Hail, king of the Jews!' and slapping him in the face."

"Daughters of Zion, come and see King Solomon, wearing the diadem with which his mother crowned him on his wedding day, on the day of his heart's joy."

Wisdom from the Saints

"Love is proved by deeds, and the more difficult the deeds, the greater the love." - St. Teresa of Ávila

"Crown Him with your love, since He let Himself be crowned with thorns for you." - St. Augustine

Reflection

A Jewish Bridegroom was always crowned on his wedding day. In God's divine plan, the very ones who crucified Jesus were the ones to give Him His wedding crown. What the enemy tried to use for the destruction of God's Kingdom, God used for the life of the world. The world mocked Jesus, crowning Him with thorns and rejecting His kingship, yet His Kingdom is not built on power but on sacrificial love. As the Divine Bridegroom, Jesus shows us the path of authentic love, a love that is proclaimed not only through words, but most importantly through deeds, a love that desires and acts for the good of the beloved. As you contemplate this third Mystery of the Rosary, ponder Jesus as the Divine Bridegroom Who willingly accepted a wedding crown of thorns to make you His bride.

Questions for Journaling and Reflection

- Do I acknowledge Christ as King of my life in all things?

- What worldly 'crowns' do I cling to instead of His crown of love?
- How can I honor Him as my King and Bridegroom?

Rosary Prayer (One Decade)

Opening Prayer:

Come Holy Spirit, Sweet Spouse of the Blessed Virgin Mary and Spouse of my soul. Purify and prepare my heart to be a virginal womb in which Divine Love may grow. May Jesus find His place of rest and delight here in the womb of my heart. Amen.

Apostles' Creed
Our Father
3 Hail Marys

Hail Mary full of grace, the Lord is with thee. Blessed art thou amongst women and blessed is the fruit of thy womb, Jesus. Holy Mary, Mother of God, **make my heart like unto thy virginal womb**, and pray for us sinners now and at the hour of our death. Amen.

Glory Be

The Third Sorrowful Mystery: The Crowning with Thorns

Prayer: Sorrowful Mother, be with me as I meditate on the Bridegroom's willing acceptance of a crown of thorns as His wedding crown so that I might be His bride for all eternity. In your care, may my bridal heart flourish in the fertile soil of suffering. And, through your intercession, may I one day see Him in His crown of glory.

"Daughters of Zion, come and see King Solomon, wearing the diadem with which his mother crowned him on his wedding day, on the day of his heart's joy." Song of Songs 3:11

Our Father, 10 Hail Marys

Hail Mary full of grace, the Lord is with thee. Blessed art thou amongst women and blessed is the fruit of thy womb, Jesus. Holy Mary, Mother of God, **make**

my heart like unto thy virginal womb, and pray for us sinners now and at the hour of our death. Amen.

Glory Be, Fatima Prayer

Closing Prayer:

Jesus, Sweet Spouse of my soul, I open the womb of my heart to You. Come and enter Your enclosed garden with the same incarnate love with which You entered the immaculate womb of Your Blessed Mother. In me, with me, and through me, bring the joy of Your Divine Love to birth again today. Amen.

Jésus portant sa croix, La Vierge sur le chemin du Calvaire (1856)
Émile Signol (French, 1804-1892)

Day 17 - The Sorrowful Mysteries
The Fourth Sorrowful Mystery:
The Carrying of the Cross

Scripture: John 19: 16-17, Luke 23:26-29

"So at that Pilate handed him over to them to be crucified. They then took charge of Jesus, and carrying his own cross he went out to the Place of the Skull or, as it is called in Hebrew, Golgotha"

"As they led him away, they seized a man, Simon of Cyrene, who was coming from the country, and they laid the cross on him, and made him carry it behind Jesus. A great number of the people followed him, and among them were women who were beating their breasts and wailing for him. But Jesus turned to them and said, 'Daughters of Jerusalem, do not weep for me, but weep for yourselves and for your children. For the days are surely coming when they will say, 'Blessed are the barren, and the wombs that never bore, and the breasts that never nursed."

Wisdom from the Saints

"The Bride must resemble her Betrothed."
~St. Faustina

"We must carry our cross in love, and our cross will carry us." ~St. Francis de Sales

Reflection

Jesus labors under the weight of the cross as a woman labors to birth a new child into the world. Because their hearts are one, Mary's heart is crushed under the weight of His cross, too. Together they are laboring to birth redemption and reconciliation into our fallen world. Their suffering is reparation and healing for the rupture Adam and Eve's sin caused in man's relationship with the Father. The Bridegroom painstakingly climbs the "mountain of myrrh" (Song of Songs 4:6) carrying His own marriage bed upon His back.

Our first instinct is to avoid or find quick relief for our pains. Jesus and Mary teach us a new way, a holy way, a redemptive way for all the pains in our lives, especially those that seem to have no solution. If we accept our crosses and carry them with Him, we will discover that every burden united with Christ becomes a gift of love. The Bridegroom asks each of us, "Will you follow me to the mountain of myrrh, the hill of frankincense?" We do not choose suffering for suffering's sake, but we do have the choice to give our "fiat" to the suffering that comes our way, accepting it as a gift of love to be united with Christ's own gift of love.

Questions for Journaling and Reflection

- What crosses am I carrying right now that I want to invite the Bridegroom to carry with me?
- How can I draw closer to Mother Mary in my suffering?
- Reflect on your thoughts and feelings about the labor pains of birthing love.

Rosary Prayer (One Decade)

Opening Prayer:

Come Holy Spirit, Sweet Spouse of the Blessed Virgin Mary and Spouse of my soul. Purify and prepare my heart to be a virginal womb in which Divine Love may grow. May Jesus find His place of rest and delight here in the womb of my heart. Amen.

Apostles' Creed
Our Father
3 Hail Marys

Hail Mary full of grace, the Lord is with thee. Blessed art thou amongst women and blessed is the fruit of thy womb, Jesus. Holy Mary, Mother of God, **make my heart like unto thy virginal womb**, and pray for us sinners now and at the hour of our death. Amen.

Glory Be

The Fourth Sorrowful Mystery: The Carrying of the Cross

Prayer: Sorrowful Mother, just as my Jesus willingly accepted the burden of the Cross for me, help me to accept my cross with trustful abandonment to the Father's will. May I have eyes to see the cross He has chosen for me as His gift of love. I desire to walk the Way of the Cross with you and Jesus, for this is the path to a purified heart, a heart that has been transformed into a womb like unto yours.

> *"Before the dawn wind rises, before the shadows flee, I will go to the mountain of myrrh, to the hill of frankincense."* (*Song of Songs* 4:6)

Our Father, 10 Hail Marys

Hail Mary full of grace, the Lord is with thee. Blessed art thou amongst women and blessed is the fruit of thy womb, Jesus. Holy Mary, Mother of God, **make my heart like unto thy virginal womb**, and pray for us sinners now and at the hour of our death. Amen.

Glory Be, Fatima Prayer

Closing Prayer:

Jesus, Sweet Spouse of my soul, I open the womb of my heart to You. Come and enter Your enclosed garden with the same incarnate love with which You entered the immaculate womb of Your Blessed Mother. In me, with me, and through me, bring the joy of Your Divine Love to birth again today. Amen.

Crucifixion (mid-16th century)
Marcellus Coffermans (ca. 1520-1578)

Day 18 - The Sorrowful Mysteries
The Fifth Sorrowful Mystery:
The Crucifixion of Jesus

Scripture: John 19: 25-37

"Near the cross of Jesus stood his mother and his mother's sister, Mary the wife of Clopas, and Mary of Magdala. Seeing his mother and the disciple whom he loved standing near her, Jesus said to his mother, 'Woman, this is your son.' Then to the disciple he said, 'This is your mother.' And from that hour the disciple took her into his home. After this, Jesus knew that everything had now been completed and, so that the scripture should be completely fulfilled, he said: I am thirsty. A jar full of sour wine stood there; so, putting a sponge soaked in the wine on a hyssop stick, they held it up to his mouth. After Jesus had taken the wine he said, 'It is fulfilled'; and bowing his head he gave up his spirit. It was the Day of Preparation, and to avoid the bodies' remaining on the cross during the Sabbath - since that Sabbath was a day of special solemnity - the Jews asked Pilate to have the legs broken and the bodies taken away. Consequently the

soldiers came and broke the legs of the first man who had been crucified with him and then of the other. When they came to Jesus, they saw he was already dead, and so instead of breaking his legs one of the soldiers pierced his side with a lance; and immediately there came out blood and water. This is the evidence of one who saw it - true evidence, and he knows that what he says is true - and he gives it so that you may believe as well. Because all this happened to fulfil the words of scripture: Not one bone of his will be broken; and again, in another place scripture says: They will look to the one whom they have pierced."

Wisdom from the Saints

"The Cross is the school of love."
~ St. Maximilian Kolbe

"The Church was born from the pierced side of Christ as Eve was born from the side of Adam."
~ St. John Chrysostom
"Now we've always thought, and rightly so, of Christ the Son on the cross and the mother beneath him. But that's not the complete picture. That's not the deep understanding. Who is our Lord on the

cross? He's the new Adam. Where's the new Eve? At the foot of the cross. … If Eve became the mother of the living in the natural order, is not this woman at the foot of the cross to become another mother? And so the bridegroom looks down at the bride. He looks at his beloved. Christ looks at his Church. There is here the birth of the Church. As St. Augustine puts it, and here I am quoting him verbatim, 'The heavenly bridegroom left the heavenly chambers, with the presage of the nuptials before him. He came to the marriage bed of the cross, a bed not of pleasure, but of pain, united himself with the woman, and consummated the union forever.'"
~Ven. Fulton Sheen

Reflection

The Cross is the marriage bed of Jesus the Bridegroom. Here He gives Himself completely to His Bride. The laboring to birth Light and Love into the world is finished. As His Blood and Water flow from His Wounded Side, the Church and Her Sacraments are born; God and humanity are reconciled. And, as Scripture tells us, at the foot of the Bridegroom's Cross stands His Mother. She has labored with Him and her heart is pierced open allowing her love to flow out just as His very Life is poured out. Here, love is perfected.

The Bridegroom invites us to follow Him to the Cross, ""If anyone would come after me, let him deny himself and take up his cross and follow me." (Matthew 16:24-26). The crosses He asks us to bear, the sufferings we endure, have the potential to stretch, expand, and open our hearts just as contractions stretch and open the womb of a woman in labor. And just as a woman births new life into the world, our labor pains birth the Christ-life anew.

Questions for Journaling and Reflection

- How does contemplating the Cross deepen my love for Christ?
- What does it mean for me to be the bride for whom He willingly offered up His life?
- Does thinking of my sufferings as "labor pains" change how I feel about the crosses I bear?

Rosary Prayer (One Decade)

Opening Prayer: Come Holy Spirit, Sweet Spouse of the Blessed Virgin Mary and Spouse of my soul. Purify and prepare my heart to be a virginal womb in which Divine Love may grow. May Jesus find His place of rest and delight here in the womb of my heart. Amen.

Apostles' Creed
Our Father
3 Hail Marys

Hail Mary full of grace, the Lord is with thee. Blessed art thou amongst women and blessed is the fruit of thy womb, Jesus. Holy Mary, Mother of God, **make my heart like unto thy virginal womb**, and pray for us sinners now and at the hour of our death. Amen.

Glory Be
The Fifth Sorrowful Mystery: The Crucifixion of Jesus

Prayer: Sorrowful Mother, together let us stand at the foot of the Bridegroom's Cross and be His succor as He gives His life for the life of His Bride. May my heart be a purified and empty chalice into which His Precious Blood and Living Water may flow.

Our Father, 10 Hail Marys

Hail Mary full of grace, the Lord is with thee. Blessed art thou amongst women and blessed is the fruit of thy womb, Jesus. Holy Mary, Mother of God, **make my heart like unto thy virginal womb**, and pray for us sinners now and at the hour of our death. Amen.

Glory Be, Fatima Prayer

Closing Prayer:

Jesus, Sweet Spouse of my soul, I open the womb of my heart to You. Come and enter Your enclosed garden with the same incarnate love with which You entered the immaculate womb of Your Blessed Mother. In me, with me, and through me, bring the joy of Your Divine Love to birth again today. Amen.

Day 19 - Praying the Full Sorrowful Mysteries of the Rosary

Reflection

The Sorrowful Mysteries are the consummation of the sacrificial love of Christ the Bridegroom and Mary, Mother and Bride. Throughout the painful events remembered in the Sorrowful Mysteries, Jesus and Mary suffer to give birth to our new life. We, too, must suffer to bring the Light and Love of Christ into the darkness of our world. Jesus and Mary teach us through our meditation on their Sorrowful Mysteries that in our personal sorrowful mysteries we do not suffer alone. They have gone before us and they go with us.

Questions for Journaling and Reflection

- Which Sorrowful Mystery most moved my heart this week?
- How can I more freely and totally receive Christ's sacrificial love?

- How can I respond with deeper love and fidelity as his bride?
- Write a prayer to Mother Mary asking her help to endure the labor pains of love.

Praying the Rosary

The Sorrowful Mysteries

Opening Prayer:

Come Holy Spirit, Sweet Spouse of the Blessed Virgin Mary and Spouse of my soul. Purify and prepare my heart to be a virginal womb in which Divine Love may grow. May Jesus find His place of rest and delight here in the womb of my heart. Amen.

Apostles' Creed
Our Father
3 Hail Marys

Hail Mary full of grace, the Lord is with thee. Blessed art thou amongst women and blessed is the fruit of thy womb, Jesus. Holy Mary, Mother of God, **make**

my heart like unto thy virginal womb, and pray for us sinners now and at the hour of our death. Amen.

Glory Be

The First Sorrowful Mystery: The Agony in the Garden

Prayer: Sorrowful Mother, pray for me and teach me fearless trust in the will of God. May I comfort Jesus in His agony by allowing my heart to be conformed to your Immaculate Heart so as to be a place of rest for Him. May the Father's will and not mine be done.

Our Father, 10 Hail Marys

Hail Mary full of grace, the Lord is with thee. Blessed art thou amongst women and blessed is the fruit of thy womb, Jesus. Holy Mary, Mother of God, **make my heart like unto thy virginal womb**, and pray for us sinners now and at the hour of our death. Amen. Glory Be, Fatima Prayer

The Second Sorrowful Mystery: The Scourging at the Pillar

Prayer: Sorrowful Mother, together let us hold and anoint the beaten Body of our Beloved Jesus. May my loving attentiveness to Him in His time of excruciating suffering be a soothing balm.

Our Father, 10 Hail Marys

Hail Mary full of grace, the Lord is with thee. Blessed art thou amongst women and blessed is the fruit of thy womb, Jesus. Holy Mary, Mother of God, **make my heart like unto thy virginal womb**, and pray for us sinners now and at the hour of our death. Amen. Glory Be, Fatima Prayer

The Third Sorrowful Mystery: The Crowning with Thorns

Prayer: Sorrowful Mother, be with me as I meditate on the Bridegroom's willing acceptance of a crown of thorns as His wedding crown so that I might be His bride for all eternity. In your care, may my bridal heart flourish in the fertile soil of suffering. And through your intercession, may I one day see Him in His crown of glory.

Our Father, 10 Hail Marys

Hail Mary full of grace, the Lord is with thee. Blessed art thou amongst women and blessed is the fruit of thy womb, Jesus. Holy Mary, Mother of God, **make my heart like unto thy virginal womb,** and pray for us sinners now and at the hour of our death. Amen.

Glory Be, Fatima Prayer

The Fourth Sorrowful Mystery: The Carrying of the Cross

Prayer: Sorrowful Mother, just as my Jesus willingly accepted the burden of the Cross for me, help me to accept my cross with trustful abandonment to the Father's will. May I have eyes to see the cross He has chosen for me as His gift of love. I desire to walk the Way of the Cross with you and Jesus for this is the path to a purified heart.

Our Father, 10 Hail Marys

Hail Mary full of grace, the Lord is with thee. Blessed art thou amongst women and blessed is the fruit of thy womb, Jesus. Holy Mary, Mother of God, **make my heart like unto thy virginal womb**, and pray for us sinners now and at the hour of our death. Amen.

Glory Be, Fatima Prayer

The Fifth Sorrowful Mystery: The Crucifixion of Jesus

Prayer: Sorrowful Mother, together let us stand at the foot of the Bridegroom's Cross and be His succor as He gives His life for the life of His Bride. May my heart be a purified and empty chalice into which His Precious Blood and Living Water may flow.

Our Father, 10 Hail Marys
Hail Mary full of grace, the Lord is with thee. Blessed art thou amongst women and blessed is the fruit of thy womb, Jesus. Holy Mary, Mother of God, **make**

my heart like unto thy virginal womb, and pray for us sinners now and at the hour of our death. Amen.

Glory Be, Fatima Prayer

Closing Prayer:

Jesus, Sweet Spouse of my soul, I open the womb of my heart to You. Come and enter Your enclosed garden with the same incarnate love with which You entered the immaculate womb of Your Blessed Mother. In me, with me, and through me, bring the joy of Your Divine Love to birth again today. Amen.

Hail Holy Queen

Jesus og Maria (1608 – 1671)
Gerhard Altzenbach (German, 1609-1672)

The Glorious Mysteries

Risen Christ appears to his Mother (1600, Italy)

Daniele Monteleone (ca. late 16th – early 17th century)

Day 20 - The Glorious Mysteries
The First Glorious Mystery:
The Resurrection of Jesus

Scripture: John 20: 11-29

"But Mary was standing outside near the tomb, weeping. Then, as she wept, she stooped to look inside, and saw two angels in white sitting where the body of Jesus had been, one at the head, the other at the feet. They said, 'Woman, why are you weeping?' 'They have taken my Lord away,' she replied, 'and I don't know where they have put him.' As she said this she turned round and saw Jesus standing there, though she did not realise that it was Jesus. Jesus said to her, 'Woman, why are you weeping? Who are you looking for?' Supposing him to be the gardener, she said, 'Sir, if you have taken him away, tell me where you have put him, and I will go and remove him.' Jesus said, 'Mary!' She turned round then and said to him in Hebrew, 'Rabbuni!' - which means Master. Jesus said to her, 'Do not cling to me, because I have not yet ascended to the Father. But go to the brothers, and tell them: I am ascending to my Father and your Father, to my

155

God and your God.' So Mary of Magdala told the disciples, 'I have seen the Lord,' and that he had said these things to her."

Wisdom from the Saints

"The resurrection of Jesus Christ is the ultimate proof of God's power to redeem and transform all things." ~ Saint Athanasius

"Easter is a season of profound transformation, a time when the old gives way to the new and the broken is made whole. It is a reminder that God's power is made perfect in weakness, and that His grace is sufficient for all our needs."
~ Saint Faustina Kowalska

Reflection

To worldly eyes, the story ended with the Fifth Sorrowful Mystery. Jesus was dead and placed in the tomb. But, with eyes of faith, we know that just as new life begins hidden in a woman's womb, new life also begins hidden in the darkness of the tomb. Likewise, we can be assured that the new Christ-life buried within each of us begins in the silent and secret depths of our hearts, and by His grace, it will surely grow. Life in union with the Divine Bridegroom has no endings, only new beginnings. His love is stronger than death!

Questions for Journaling and Reflection

- Where do I need Christ's resurrection power in my life today?
- Read the Scripture passage above again, imagining that you are Mary Magdalene. How would you feel, what would you say and do when Jesus reveals Himself to you?
- Where have I seen Christ bring wholeness where there was only brokenness, new life where once there was death?

Rosary Prayer (One Decade)

Opening Prayer:

Come Holy Spirit, Sweet Spouse of the Blessed Virgin Mary and Spouse of my soul. Purify and prepare my heart to be a virginal womb in which Divine Love may grow. May Jesus find His place of rest and delight here in the womb of my heart. Amen.

Apostles' Creed
Our Father
3 Hail Marys

Hail Mary full of grace, the Lord is with thee. Blessed art thou amongst women and blessed is the fruit of thy womb, Jesus. Holy Mary, Mother of God, **make my heart like unto thy virginal womb**, and pray for us sinners now and at the hour of our death. Amen.

Glory Be, Fatima Prayer

The First Glorious Mystery: The Resurrection of Jesus

Prayer: Mary, Mother of the Resurrected Bridegroom, when my heart feels like a tomb, please remind me that the power that raised your Son, Christ, from the dead lives in me. It is in the tomb that new life in Christ blooms. Come Holy Spirit and make my heart like unto the garden of His Resurrection.

> *"On my bed, at night, I sought him whom my heart loves. I sought but did not find him. So I will rise and go through the City; in the streets and the squares I will seek him whom my heart loves. ... I sought but did not find him. The watchmen came upon me on their rounds in the City: 'Have you seen him whom my heart loves?' Scarcely had I passed them then I found him whom my heart loves. I held him fast, nor would I let him go till I had brought him into my mother's house, into the room of her who conceived me." ~ Song of Songs 3:1-4*

Our Father, 10 Hail Marys

Hail Mary full of grace, the Lord is with thee. Blessed art thou amongst women and blessed is the fruit of thy womb, Jesus. Holy Mary, Mother of God, **make my heart like unto thy virginal womb**, and pray for us sinners now and at the hour of our death. Amen.

Glory Be, Fatima Prayer

Closing Prayer:

Jesus, Sweet Spouse of my soul, I open the womb of my heart to You. Come and enter Your enclosed garden with the same incarnate love with which You entered the immaculate womb of Your Blessed Mother. In me, with me, and through me, bring the joy of Your Divine Love to birth again today. Amen.

Apotheosis of Christ (1894)

Ernst Friedrich von Liphart (Russian, 1847–1932)

Day 21 - The Glorious Mysteries
The Second Glorious Mystery:
The Ascension

Scripture: Luke 24: 44-53

"Then he told them, 'This is what I meant when I said, while I was still with you, that everything written about me in the Law of Moses, in the Prophets and in the Psalms, was destined to be fulfilled.' He then opened their minds to understand the scriptures, and he said to them, 'So it is written that the Christ would suffer and on the third day rise from the dead, and that, in his name, repentance for the forgiveness of sins would be preached to all nations, beginning from Jerusalem. You are witnesses to this. 'And now I am sending upon you what the Father has promised. Stay in the city, then, until you are clothed with the power from on high.' Then he took them out as far as the outskirts of Bethany, and raising his hands he blessed them. Now as he blessed them, he withdrew from them and was carried up to heaven. They worshipped him and then went back to Jerusalem full of joy;

and they were continually in the Temple praising God.'"

Wisdom from the Saints

"While in heaven, He does not cease to be present with us on earth." ~St. Leo the Great

"Jesus has gone to prepare a place for us, and we should long for heaven." ~St. Augustine

"The Church is a mother, not only bringing forth children but nourishing them with her own milk. She brings them to maturity through the preaching of the word." ~ St. John Chrysostom, Homily on Matthew 16

Reflection

The Bridegroom ascends, not to leave His Bride, but to prepare a dwelling place for Her in eternity. His promise fills us with longing: our home is not here but with Him, rejoicing forever at the Heavenly Wedding Feast. In our waiting and our longing to be reunited with Jesus, He does not leave us orphans. At the foot of His Cross, His Church was born. Mary, through her co-suffering, was invited into this birth of the Church in a particular way, as she is at the heart of the Church, our Mother. As Mother, the Church gives spiritual birth to the children of God, and as members of the Church, we are called to give spiritual birth to Christ within our own lives. Mary our Mother accompanies us and intercedes for us as we journey on towards our true home where our Bridegroom and King awaits.

Questions for Journaling and Reflection

- How does the hope of heaven influence the way I live each day?
- Where am I too attached to the things of this world?
- How does Christ's promise of preparing a place for me give me peace?

Rosary Prayer (One Decade)

Opening Prayer:

Come Holy Spirit, Sweet Spouse of the Blessed Virgin Mary and Spouse of my soul. Purify and prepare my heart to be a virginal womb in which Divine Love may grow. May Jesus find His place of rest and delight here in the womb of my heart. Amen.

Apostles' Creed
Our Father
3 Hail Marys

Hail Mary full of grace, the Lord is with thee. Blessed art thou amongst women and blessed is the fruit of thy womb, Jesus. Holy Mary, Mother of God, **make my heart like unto thy virginal womb**, and pray for us sinners now and at the hour of our death. Amen.

Glory Be, Fatima Prayer

The Second Glorious Mystery: The Ascension of Jesus

Prayer: Raise me up, my Jesus, above the miry bog of sin; above my foolish and base desires; above my pride and vanity; raise me up to where You are. May I always seek what is above - You and the Eternal Wedding Feast.

Our Father, 10 Hail Marys

Hail Mary full of grace, the Lord is with thee. Blessed art thou amongst women and blessed is the fruit of thy womb, Jesus. Holy Mary, Mother of God, **make my heart like unto thy virginal womb**, and pray for us sinners now and at the hour of our death. Amen.

Glory Be, Fatima Prayer

Closing Prayer: Jesus, Sweet Spouse of my soul, I open the womb of my heart to You. Come and enter Your enclosed garden with the same incarnate love with which You entered the immaculate womb of Your Blessed Mother. In me, with me, and through me, bring the joy of Your Divine Love to birth again today. Amen.

The Pentecost (1500)
Jean Poyet (ca. 1445-1503)

Day 22 - The Glorious Mysteries
The Third Glorious Mystery:
Pentecost - the Coming of the Holy Spirit

Scripture: Acts 2: 1-17

"When Pentecost day came round, they had all met together, when suddenly there came from heaven a sound as of a violent wind which filled the entire house in which they were sitting; and there appeared to them tongues as of fire; these separated and came to rest on the head of each of them. They were all filled with the Holy Spirit and began to speak different languages as the Spirit gave them power to express themselves. Now there were devout men living in Jerusalem from every nation under heaven, and at this sound they all assembled, and each one was bewildered to hear these men speaking his own language. They were amazed and astonished. 'Surely,' they said, 'all these men speaking are Galileans? How does it happen that each of us hears them in his own native language? Parthians, Medes and Elamites; people from Mesopotamia, Judaea and Cappadocia, Pontus and Asia, Phrygia and Pamphylia,

Egypt and the parts of Libya round Cyrene; residents of Rome- Jews and proselytes alike - Cretans and Arabs, we hear them preaching in our own language about the marvels of God.' Everyone was amazed and perplexed; they asked one another what it all meant. Some, however, laughed it off. 'They have been drinking too much new wine,' they said. Then Peter stood up with the Eleven and addressed them in a loud voice: 'Men of Judaea, and all you who live in Jerusalem, make no mistake about this, but listen carefully to what I say. These men are not drunk, as you imagine; why, it is only the third hour of the day. On the contrary, this is what the prophet was saying: In the last days - the Lord declares - I shall pour out my Spirit on all humanity. Your sons and daughters shall prophesy, your young people shall see visions, your old people dream dreams."

Wisdom from the Saints

"Without the Holy Spirit, God is far away. With the Spirit, the Gospel is the power of life." ~St. Athanasius

"The Holy Spirit is the bond of love between the Father and the Son - and He fills our hearts with the same divine love." ~St. Augustine

Reflection

At Pentecost, Mary is once again overshadowed by the Holy Spirit and filled with the Divine Presence. This time she is not alone; the Apostles are with her and they too are overshadowed and filled with the Holy Spirit. The Spirit of Love, the very love shared between Father and Son, is poured into the heart of the Church. It is only by the power of this same Spirit filling us that we are able to conceive the Christ-life within the womb of our hearts. The Holy Spirit gives us courage and strength to bring Christ to the world.

Questions for Journaling and Reflection

- How open am I to the power of the Holy Spirit in my life?
- Where in my life do I most need the Spirit's courage, strength, or wisdom?
- Like Mary at the Annunciation and Pentecost, how is God inviting me to let the spirit 'overshadow' me so I can share Christ with others?

Rosary Prayer (One Decade)

Opening Prayer:

Come Holy Spirit, Sweet Spouse of the Blessed Virgin Mary and Spouse of my soul. Purify and prepare my heart to be a virginal womb in which Divine Love may grow. May Jesus find His place of rest and delight here in the womb of my heart. Amen.

Apostles' Creed
Our Father
3 Hail Marys

Hail Mary full of grace, the Lord is with thee. Blessed art thou amongst women and blessed is the fruit of thy womb, Jesus. Holy Mary, Mother of God, **make my heart like unto thy virginal womb**, and pray for us sinners now and at the hour of our death. Amen.

Glory Be, Fatima Prayer

The Third Glorious Mystery: Pentecost - the Coming of the Holy Spirit

Prayer: Come Holy Spirit and breathe over my garden heart. May my life blossom with flowers of charity and holiness and may the sweet scent of the Bridegroom's love pour forth from within me.

"Awake, north wind, come, wind of the south! Breathe over my garden, to spread its sweet smell around. Let my Beloved come into his garden, let him taste its rarest fruits." ~Song of Songs 4:16

Our Father, 10 Hail Marys

Hail Mary full of grace, the Lord is with thee. Blessed art thou amongst women and blessed is the fruit of thy womb, Jesus. Holy Mary, Mother of God, **make my heart like unto thy virginal womb**, and pray for us sinners now and at the hour of our death. Amen.

Glory Be, Fatima Prayer

Closing Prayer:

Jesus, Sweet Spouse of my soul, I open the womb of my heart to You. Come and enter Your enclosed garden with the same incarnate love with which You entered the immaculate womb of Your Blessed Mother. In me, with me, and through me, bring the joy of Your Divine Love to birth again today. Amen.

Assumption of the Virgin (1637)

Guido Reni (1575-1642)

Day 23 - The Glorious Mysteries
The Fourth Glorious Mystery:
The Assumption of Mary

Scripture: Revelation 11:19 - 12:6

"Then the sanctuary of God in heaven opened, and the ark of the covenant could be seen inside it. Then came flashes of lightning, peals of thunder and an earthquake and violent hail. Now a great sign appeared in heaven: a woman, robed with the sun, standing on the moon, and on her head a crown of twelve stars. She was pregnant, and in labour, crying aloud in the pangs of childbirth. Then a second sign appeared in the sky: there was a huge red dragon with seven heads and ten horns, and each of the seven heads crowned with a coronet. Its tail swept a third of the stars from the sky and hurled them to the ground, and the dragon stopped in front of the woman as she was at the point of giving birth, so that it could eat the child as soon as it was born. The woman was delivered of a boy, the son who was to rule all the nations with an iron sceptre, and the child was taken straight up to God and to his throne, while the woman escaped into

the desert, where God had prepared a place for her to be looked after for twelve hundred and sixty days."

Wisdom from the Saints

"Mary's Assumption into heaven is the greatest honor of our human nature." ~St. John Damascene

"Taken up into Heaven, Mary shows us the way to God, the way to Heaven, the way to life. She shows it to her children baptized in Christ and to all people of good will." ~St. John Paul II

"I wish I could help people understand that the Eucharist is a heaven, given that 'heaven is only a tabernacle without doors, a Eucharist without veils, a never-ending Communion.'" ~St. Teresa of Jesus of the Andes

Reflection

The vision in Revelation of the "woman robed with the sun" reveals Mary as the Ark of the New Covenant and the radiant Bride adorned for her Bridegroom. Just as the Ark in the Old Testament carried God's presence, Mary carried within her the living Word, Jesus Christ. Because of this unique role, her body was preserved from corruption and assumed into heaven.

The Assumption is not only a truth about Mary, but also a promise for us. She goes before us as the first to fully share in her Son's victory over death. The Bridegroom, who once entered her womb, now receives her whole being into glory. As His faithful Bride, she models the destiny that awaits the entire Church: eternal union with Christ, body and soul.

The One born of Mary has come not only to redeem us but to bring us into the fullness of His Kingdom. Mary's Assumption strengthens our hope. What Christ has done for her, He longs to do for us. And His ardent desire caused Him to give us the gift of the Holy Eucharist so we might have a foretaste of the glorious destiny He has in store for us. In the Eucharist, heaven enters the womb of our hearts. May our faithful reception of Christ's Body and Blood increase our longing to see Him and His Mother face to face.

Questions for Journaling and Reflection

- How does Mary's Assumption strengthen my hope in Christ's promise of eternal life, both body and soul?
- In what ways do I see Mary as a model of faithful love and total union with her Bridegroom?
- How can I live with greater awareness that my ultimate destiny is to be with Christ in glory?

Rosary Prayer (One Decade)

Opening Prayer:

Come Holy Spirit, Sweet Spouse of the Blessed Virgin Mary and Spouse of my soul. Purify and prepare my heart to be a virginal womb in which Divine Love may grow. May Jesus find His place of rest and delight here in the womb of my heart. Amen.

Apostles' Creed
Our Father
3 Hail Marys

Hail Mary full of grace, the Lord is with thee. Blessed art thou amongst women and blessed is the fruit of thy womb, Jesus. Holy Mary, Mother of God, **make my heart like unto thy virginal womb**, and pray for us sinners now and at the hour of our death. Amen.

Glory Be, Fatima Prayer

The Fourth Glorious Mystery: The Assumption of Mary

Prayer: My Jesus, I do believe that Mary's destiny is my destiny, too. Grant me the grace to live rooted in the truth that my body is Your temple and my destiny is Heaven where I will live eternally in union with You. May I enflesh Your love, here and now, for the life of the world.

> *"There are sixty queens and eighty concubines (and countless maidens). But my dove is unique, mine, unique and perfect. She is the darling of her mother, the favourite of the one who bore her. The maidens saw her, and proclaimed her blessed, queens and concubines sang her praises: 'Who is this arising like the dawn, fair as the moon, resplendent as the sun, terrible as an army with banners?'" Song of Songs 6:8-9*

Our Father, 10 Hail Marys

Hail Mary full of grace, the Lord is with thee. Blessed art thou amongst women and blessed is the fruit of thy womb, Jesus. Holy Mary, Mother of God, **make my heart like unto thy virginal womb**, and pray for us sinners now and at the hour of our death. Amen.

Glory Be, Fatima Prayer

Closing Prayer:

Jesus, Sweet Spouse of my soul, I open the womb of my heart to You. Come and enter Your enclosed garden with the same incarnate love with which You entered the immaculate womb of Your Blessed Mother. In me, with me, and through me, bring the joy of Your Divine Love to birth again today. Amen.

Coronation of the Virgin (ca. 1400s)

Master of the Beffi Triptych

Day 24 - The Glorious Mysteries

The Fifth Glorious Mystery:
The Coronation of Mary

Scripture: Revelation 12: 1-17

"Now a great sign appeared in heaven: a woman, robed with the sun, standing on the moon, and on her head a crown of twelve stars. She was pregnant, and in labour, crying aloud in the pangs of childbirth. Then a second sign appeared in the sky: there was a huge red dragon with seven heads and ten horns, and each of the seven heads crowned with a coronet. Its tail swept a third of the stars from the sky and hurled them to the ground, and the dragon stopped in front of the woman as she was at the point of giving birth, so that it could eat the child as soon as it was born. The woman was delivered of a boy, the son who was to rule all the nations with an iron sceptre, and the child was taken straight up to God and to his throne, while the woman escaped into the desert, where God had prepared a place for her to be looked after for twelve *hundred and sixty days.*"

Wisdom from the Saints

"Mary is the Queen of heaven and earth because she is the Mother of the King of kings." ~ St. Alphonsus Liguori

"We never give more honor to Jesus than when we honor His Mother." ~ St. Louis de Montfort

"What can be more sweet, brethren, than to think of Mary and to honor her name? She is the mother of mercy, bringing forth the life of grace in us."
~ St. Bernard of Clairvaux, Homilies in Praise of the Virgin Mother

Reflection

The Bridegroom crowns his Bride, Mary, as Queen of heaven and earth. She reigns not as a distant sovereign, but as a loving Mother, interceding for her children and gently leading us into the Kingdom of her Son. A mother is responsible for nurturing, nourishing, protecting, and forming the new life entrusted to her. God has entrusted each of us with seeds of the Christ-life buried within the womb of our hearts. Mother Mary will teach us how to nurture and nourish, protect and form, and then to give birth to the life and love of her Son. Through all the trials and labor pains of birthing Love anew, let us keep our eyes fixed on what is above, our Queen Mother.

Questions for Journaling and Reflection

- What does it mean for me to have Mary as my Queen and Mother?
- How can I entrust myself more fully to her maternal intercession?
- In what ways do I need Mother Mary's help so I can better nurture the Christ-life within me?

Rosary Prayer (One Decade)

Opening Prayer:

Come Holy Spirit, Sweet Spouse of the Blessed Virgin Mary and Spouse of my soul. Purify and prepare my heart to be a virginal womb in which Divine Love may grow. May Jesus find His place of rest and delight here in the womb of my heart. Amen.

Apostles' Creed
Our Father
3 Hail Marys

Hail Mary full of grace, the Lord is with thee. Blessed art thou amongst women and blessed is the fruit of thy womb, Jesus. Holy Mary, Mother of God, **make my heart like unto thy virginal womb**, and pray for us sinners now and at the hour of our death. Amen.

Glory Be, Fatima Prayer

The Fifth Glorious Mystery: The Coronation of Mary

Prayer: Holy Mary, Queen of Heaven, I enthrone you as Queen of my heart. Reign in my life and rule me with your tenderness and wisdom. Through your prayers and guidance, may I arrive safely in Heaven to see you and my Beloved Jesus face to face.

"Who is this coming up from the desert leaning
 on her Beloved?
I awakened you under the apple tree, there where
 your mother conceived you, there where she
 who gave birth to you conceived you.
Set me like a seal on your heart, like a seal on your
 arm. For love is strong as Death, jealousy relentless as Sheol. The flash of it is a flash of
 fire, a flame of Yahweh himself.
Love no flood can quench, no torrents drown."
 Song of Songs 8:5-7

Our Father, 10 Hail Marys

Hail Mary full of grace, the Lord is with thee. Blessed
art thou amongst women and blessed is the fruit of
thy womb, Jesus. Holy Mary, Mother of God, **make
my heart like unto thy virginal womb**, and pray for
us sinners now and at the hour of our death. Amen.

Glory Be, Fatima Prayer

Closing Prayer:

Jesus, Sweet Spouse of my soul, I open the womb of my heart to You. Come and enter Your enclosed garden with the same incarnate love with which You entered the immaculate womb of Your Blessed Mother. In me, with me, and through me, bring the joy of Your Divine Love to birth again today. Amen.

Day 25 - Praying the Full Glorious Mysteries of the Rosary

Reflection

The Glorious Mysteries remind us of the victory of Christ, the faithfulness of Mary, and the promise of eternal union. Our journey with Jesus and Mary does not end here. The transformation of our hearts into purified receptive wombs like unto Mary's virginal womb is not complete. Remember, with Jesus the Bridegroom there are no endings, only new beginnings! The work of becoming true icons of His Love takes a lifetime. Let us persevere in praying the Rosary and walking hand in hand with Mary, Mother and Bride, as she leads us Home. The One Whom our souls are seeking awaits us.

Questions for Journaling and Reflection

- How have I grown in intimacy with Christ the Bridegroom through these prayers and reflections?
- Which Mystery has most transformed my heart during these weeks of prayer?
- Write a prayer of gratitude to Jesus and Mary for the gift of the Rosary.

Praying the Rosary

The Glorious Mysteries

Opening Prayer:

Come Holy Spirit, Sweet Spouse of the Blessed Virgin Mary and Spouse of my soul. Purify and prepare my heart to be a virginal womb in which Divine Love may grow. May Jesus find His place of rest and delight here in the womb of my heart. Amen.

Apostles' Creed
Our Father

3 Hail Marys

Hail Mary full of grace, the Lord is with thee. Blessed art thou amongst women and blessed is the fruit of thy womb, Jesus. Holy Mary, Mother of God, **make my heart like unto thy virginal womb**, and pray for us sinners now and at the hour of our death. Amen.

Glory Be, Fatima Prayer

The First Glorious Mystery: The Resurrection of Jesus

Prayer: Mary, Mother of the Resurrected Bridegroom, when my heart feels like a tomb, please remind me that the power that raised your Son, Christ, from the dead lives in me. It is in the tomb that new life in Christ blooms. Come Holy Spirit and make my heart like unto the garden of His Resurrection.

Our Father, 10 Hail Marys

Hail Mary full of grace, the Lord is with thee. Blessed art thou amongst women and blessed is the fruit of thy womb, Jesus. Holy Mary, Mother of God, **make my heart like unto thy virginal womb**, and pray for us sinners now and at the hour of our death. Amen.

Glory Be, Fatima Prayer

The Second Glorious Mystery: The Ascension of Jesus

Prayer: Raise me up, my Jesus, above the miry bog of sin; above my foolish and base desires; above my pride and vanity; raise me up to where You are. May I always seek what is above - You and the Eternal Wedding Feast.

Our Father, 10 Hail Marys

Hail Mary full of grace, the Lord is with thee. Blessed art thou amongst women and blessed is the fruit of thy womb, Jesus. Holy Mary, Mother of God, **make my heart like unto thy virginal womb**, and pray for us sinners now and at the hour of our death. Amen. Glory Be, Fatima Prayer

The Third Glorious Mystery: Pentecost - the Coming of the Holy Spirit

Prayer: Come Holy Spirit and breathe over my garden heart. May my life blossom with flowers of charity and holiness and may the sweet scent of the Bridegroom's love pour forth from within me.

Our Father, 10 Hail Marys

Hail Mary full of grace, the Lord is with thee. Blessed art thou amongst women and blessed is the fruit of thy womb, Jesus. Holy Mary, Mother of God, **make my heart like unto thy virginal womb**, and pray for us sinners now and at the hour of our death. Amen.

Glory Be, Fatima Prayer

The Fourth Glorious Mystery: The Assumption of Mary

Prayer: My Jesus, I do believe that Mary's destiny is my destiny, too. Grant me the grace to live rooted in the truth that my body is Your temple and my destiny is Heaven where I will live eternally in union with You. May I enflesh Your love, here and now, for the life of the world.

Our Father, 10 Hail Marys

Hail Mary full of grace, the Lord is with thee. Blessed art thou amongst women and blessed is the fruit of thy womb, Jesus. Holy Mary, Mother of God, **make my heart like unto thy virginal womb**, and pray for us sinners now and at the hour of our death. Amen.

Glory Be, Fatima Prayer

The Fifth Glorious Mystery: The Coronation of Mary

Prayer: Holy Mary, Queen of Heaven, I enthrone you as Queen of my heart. Reign in my life and rule me with your tenderness and wisdom. Make my heart like unto your virginal womb. Through your prayers and guidance, may I arrive safely in Heaven to see you and my Beloved Jesus face to face.

Our Father, 10 Hail Marys

Hail Mary full of grace, the Lord is with thee. Blessed art thou amongst women and blessed is the fruit of thy womb, Jesus. Holy Mary, Mother of God, **make my heart like unto thy virginal womb**, and pray for us sinners now and at the hour of our death. Amen.

Glory Be, Fatima Prayer

Closing Prayer:

Jesus, Sweet Spouse of my soul, I open the womb of my heart to you. Come and enter Your enclosed garden with the same incarnate love with which You entered the immaculate womb of Your Blessed Mother. In me, with me, and through me, bring the joy of Your Divine Love to birth again today. Amen.

Hail Holy Queen

Not the End, But A New Beginning

We have come to the end of our twenty-five day meditation on the Womb of My Heart Rosary and, yet, we know that the Bridegroom is all about newness and beginning again, "And the one who was seated on the throne said, 'See, I am making all things new'" (Revelation 21:5). My prayer for you, dear reader, is that you have been made a new creation in Christ through these prayers and reflections and that you will return to this contemplative Rosary devotional again and again, each time allowing Jesus and Mary to make your heart a little more like unto her virginal womb. The journey of becoming icons of His holiness and love does not end until He carries us over the threshold of the Father's house and we rejoice with our Blessed Mother, the saints, and angels at the eternal wedding banquet.

Together in His Heart,

Laura Ercolino,
Foundress of Hope's Garden

www.ingramcontent.com/pod-product-compliance
Lightning Source LLC
Chambersburg PA
CBHW071957090426

42740CB00011B/1984